Eucharistic Theology
Then and Now

Other volumes in this series:

THEOLOGICAL COLLECTIONS

9

EUCHARISTIC THEOLOGY THEN AND NOW

R. E. Clements

Austin Farrer

G. W. H. Lampe

C. W. Dugmore

Alf Härdelin

John Wilkinson

C. B. Naylor

LONDON

S·P:C·K

1968

First published in 1968
by S.P.C.K.
Holy Trinity Church
Marylebone Road
London N.W.1

Printed in Great Britain by
The Talbot Press (S.P.C.K.)
Saffron Walden, Essex

PUBLISHER'S NOTE

THE series in which this volume is issued is designed for the theologically literate but not specialist reader, who tries to keep up his reading on a broad front, wants to see current problems of the Church in their wider perspective, and likes to know what the specialists are interested in, but has not sufficient time at his disposal to read in depth over the whole field of theological study. It is hoped that *Theological Collections* will also be of help to the specialist in one branch of theology who wants to be generally aware of what is going on in other branches, but does not read all the journals. Each volume is planned round a selected theme. Most former numbers have contained both reprints and previously unpublished papers, but all the contributions to this present Collection have been specially written for the purpose.

There could be no more inappropriate designation of the Eucharist than that of *sacramentum unitatis*. Different thinkers have always understood it in different ways, and diversely expressed its particular significance for them. But each age seems to take a particular aspect on which to disagree. At one time it may be realism versus symbolism, at another it may be the nature of sacrifice, at a third it may be the relation between Word and Action in the sacramental whole. Much fruitless logomachy has resulted from the failure to realize that the pattern of thought within which the divines of one age argued to their diametrically-opposed conclusions was not that of an earlier or a later era, or, as Professor Lampe more simply puts it, that "Cyprian was not answering the questions of the sixteenth and later centuries". Yet the pattern of thought is of more ultimate significance than the particular theologies which arise from it. What signifies is the manner of thinking which takes some things for granted and is so curiously blind to some others, the *Zeitgeist*, the spirit of the age, which provides sufficient in common for rival theologians to argue from similar premises. It is because the *Zeitgeist* of the Patristic age was different from that of the age of the Reformation and counter-Reformation, and different again from that of our own time, that there is value in looking at a series of cross-sections of Christian history to see what kinds of eucharistic controversy characterized them. The value of the exercise will be enhanced if it begins with a consideration of the biblical roots of the whole idea of the cultic presence of God in the religion of the Old Testament and the meaning which the Eucharist may be presumed to have had for those New Testament Christians who first took part in it.

For, after all, this exercise has a practical end. Most of the symposiasts in this volume belong to the Church of England, which in the last third of the twentieth century is entering into a period of controlled experiment in the revision of its eucharistic rite. This might lead to a hardening of predetermined patterns or it might lead to a willingness mutually to study, and to attempt to understand, patterns of thought about the Eucharist with which we are not ourselves familiar. The signs are hopeful. Eucharistic thought and practice today are unusually fluid, and historical awareness may lead to flexibility in our ways of thinking. This Collection will have served its purpose if it leads to what Canon Naylor has described as "the willingness on both sides to break through the impasse created by the controversies about the eucharistic sacrifice in a penitent recogition of past theological errors and misunderstanding". If so, then perhaps a result of the rethinking occasioned by the experimental use of a new liturgy may be that at last the words *sacramentum unitatis* can be used without a wry sense of incongruity.

I

THE MEANING OF RITUAL ACTS IN ISRAELITE RELIGION

R. E. CLEMENTS

THE most fundamental question that we can ask of any religious act is "What does this mean?", and it is significant that the Old Testament itself raises this question in connection with the Feast of Passover and the offering of firstlings.[1] Ritual acts have a specific meaning attached to them, and the value of the rite is directly related to the significance which worshippers find in this meaning. We can therefore make a basic distinction between a cultic act, which is often of a symbolic or dramatic nature, and its meaning, which is conveyed through an accompanying liturgy or hymn. Outward acts are usually accompanied by verbal recitations, so that rite and word belong together. This readily makes for a further distinction between the "objective" performance of a rite and its "subjective" apprehension and appreciation. Much of our modern uncertainty regarding the significance of sacraments lies in our difficulty in relating these objective and subjective elements.

F. Gavin, in opposing the view of W. Bouset regarding the non-sacramental character of Jewish ritual washings and lustrations, argued that, for the Judaism of the New Testament period, there was no distinction between the outward performance of a rite, and its inner value for the devout worshipper.[2] Gavin connects this unity

---

[1] Ex. 12. 26 J; 13. 14 J.
[2] F. Gavin, *The Jewish Antecedents of the Christian Sacraments*, London, 1928, pp. 13f. Gavin writes, *"The implied contrast between 'inner value for the life of the devout' and outward cult practices*—to hark back to the thought of Bousset—*is* certainly *an alien category*, foreign to anything inherent in Judaism" (italics are Gavin's). The statement of W. Bousset's that is referred to is to be found in *Die Religion des Judentums im späthellenistischen Zeitalter*, revised by H. Gressmann, Tübingen, 1926, p. 199.

of outward act and inner value with the opposition of Judaism to philosophical dualism, and to its refusal to make a divorce between flesh and spirit, material object and spiritual meaning. Whilst accepting the appropriateness of much of Gavin's criticism of Bousset, the purpose of this essay is to question the rigidity with which he argues for the lack of any distinction in Judaism between outward act and inner meaning and value. We find in the Old Testament a marked tendency towards defining the meaning of cultic acts, and towards determining their inner value for the devout. Admittedly Gavin would concede this, but we must go further and recognize that the distinction between rite and meaning is made sufficiently clearly to show that these were not held to be inseparable, and that an awareness of the meaning of a rite was considered vital to its efficacy. In short there took place a theologizing and spiritualizing of the cult which did not deprive it of its sacramental character, but which very positively recognized the necessity of stating its meaning before its value and efficacy could be apprehended by the worshipping community.

1. THE BASIS OF WORSHIP IN ISRAEL

The early religion of Israel was undoubtedly cultic in its expression, since it consisted not of a self-contained body of distinctive religious ideas, but of certain cultic institutions through which Israel's communion with God was maintained. The early history of the religion of Israel is in fact the history of its cultic institutions,[3] and it is not until the Exile that a form of worship began to emerge which sought to be independent of them. The meaning of the cult is therefore a primary question which must be raised in any Old Testament theology. Through its cult Israel maintained its relationship to God, and it was through the medium of the cult that its disinctive religious ideas were preserved and handed on from one generation to the next. Membership of the religious community of Israel was expressed by participation in a particular cult, rather than by adherence to certain established beliefs, and the importance of specific religious ideas was a consequence of the interpretation of the cult.

---

[3] Cf. F. Mildenberger, *Gottes Tat im Wort. Erwägungen zur alttestamentlichen Hermeneutik als Frage nach der Einheit der Testament*, Gütersloh, 1964, p. 18.

It is therefore a fundamental aspect of Israelite religion to recognize that its cult possessed a particular meaning, for in this fact lies much of the distinctiveness of its religion. The task of uncovering this meaning, however, is a far from simple one. In the first place every effort of research into the origins of Israel's religion makes it plain that Israel's cult was not of a single, homogeneous origin, but grew up gradually over a considerable interval of time, and was drawn from a great variety of sources and religious traditions. It has long been recognized that Israel's sacrificial system and festival calendar were not derived from a single unique act of divine revelation, but grew up by Israel's adoption of rites and festivals already current in Canaan. Even such a festival as that of Passover, and such institutions as the Ark and the Tent of Meeting, all of which may have been brought into Canaan by proto-Israelite tribes at the time of their settlement in the land, cannot be shown to have had a Mosaic origin. Israel's cult, with its variety of rites and celebrations, was drawn from many sources at various times, and was only slowly welded into a unified system under the authority of the state as it emerged under David. Not until the Josianic Reform in 621 B.C., based upon the demands of Deuteronomy, do we have an attempt to provide a completely unified pattern of worship in Israel by means of a process of cultic centralization. It is significant, therefore, that Deuteronomy focuses great attention upon the element of meaning in Israel's cult.

When we ask after the meaning of ritual acts in Israel's religion we are faced with a number of important preliminary questions. Word and rite are not inseparable partners in any religious observance, and, as has long been recognized, the meaning associated with a particular rite can be changed. In fact the ritual normally remains a constant factor, whilst the meaning given to it is variable.[4] The same observance does not always have the same meaning, and can rapidly be brought into a new context, and given a quite new interpretation. This has undoubtedly taken place in the case of the celebration of Passover, and the offering of firstlings referred to at the beginning of this essay. The meanings given to them in the

---

4 For the relationship between word and rite in the cult see S. Mowinckel, *Religion und Kultus*, Göttingen, 1953, pp. 108ff., and "Kultus, religionsgeschichtlich", *Die Religion in Geschichte und Gegenwart*, 3 (3rd edn), Tübingen, 1957-62, IV, col. 1241.

relevant Old Testament passages were certainly not the original meanings which gave rise to their observance. Israel itself provided these cultic acts with a significance which was uniquely Israelite in content and character. Thus the Israelite who offered the firstlings of his herds to God came to see a very different meaning in his action from that which his Canaanite predecessor had done. How then are we to discover the meaning of Israel's cult? We may distinguish between the original meaning of a ritual act, the popular meaning attached to it when Israel borrowed it, and the particular meaning which Israelite tradition came to vest in it. The first of these meanings is no longer known to us, and can only be the subject of hypothesis on the basis of comparative evidence. Similarly the second can only be recovered with difficulty, if at all, by having regard to incidental allusions and archaic expressions which may well indicate to us an earlier level of cultic interpretation in Israel.[5] The meaning which later Israel came to attach to its worship is usually recorded for us in the Old Testament tradition, and it is this meaning which is ultimately of greatest moment for a knowledge of Israel's interpretation of its cult.

2. THE INTERPRETATION OF ISRAEL'S WORSHIP

In seeking to uncover the ways in which Israel found meaning in its cult and accepted that the due performance of its rites brought Yahweh's blessing to its members, we cannot treat individual ritual acts in isolation. The basis of worship in ancient Israel was a unity of act, symbol, and spoken word which together comprised a festival celebration. The meaning of this worship was seen in its comprehensive wholeness, rather than in the efficacy that was believed to attach to each separate rite.[6] The whole celebration had a dramatic character, and the context in which it took place gave

[5] The most probable instance of this is to be found in the interpretation of sacrificial offerings as the food of God. Cf. Lev. 21. 6, 8; 22. 25; Num. 28. 2; Ezek. 44. 7, 16; Mal. 1. 7, 12. This conception of sacrifice was undoubtedly very old, and is attested in the Ras Shamra texts. See W. Herrmann, Götterspeise und Göttertrank in Ugarit and Israel", *ZAW* 72, 1960, pp. 205-16. However R. de Vaux, *Studies in Old Testament Sacrifice*, Cardiff, 1964, pp. 40f, suggests that such a view was a later assimilation into Israel's religion from its Babylonian environment during the period of the exile.
[6] Cf. S. Mowinckel, "Drama, religionsgeschichtlich", *RGG*, 2 (2nd edn), Tübingen, 1927, cols. 2000f.

purpose and meaning to the separate parts of which it was composed. During the course of Israel's development this original unity, and dramatic character were gradually dissolved and the various rites came to be considered in greater isolation. There was a progressive spiritualization of the cult, and God was conceived in more transcendent terms, which weakened the assertions of his direct presence and activity in worship. This process was never complete, but it represented a continuing tendency during the later Old Testament period. In consequence there was a shift of emphasis away from the meaning of the cult as a whole to a concern with the meaning of its individual acts. This becomes evident in an examination of the laws regulating Israel's cult which are preserved in the Old Testament.

In seeking to interpret the meaning of the cult therefore, we must first consider its basic presuppositions. The earliest of the major law-codes of the Old Testament, the Book of the Covenant,[7] contains an injunction for the making of an altar, and of the offering of sacrifice upon it:

> An altar of earth you shall make for me and sacrifice on it your burnt offerings and your peace offerings, your sheep and your oxen; in every place where I cause my name to be remembered I will come to you and bless you (Ex. 20. 4).

It is noteworthy that instead of describing the purpose of the individual offerings given to God, there is the basic affirmation that through such worship God will himself come to Israel and bless them. Thus the divine presence is the basic presupposition of the cult, and the source of the blessing which is communicated by it. The efficacy of the acts of sacrifice is not traced back to anything in their individual symbolism or content, but to the fact that Yahweh himself is present to receive them, and to confer his power upon the worshippers. This power which was communicated through the cult consisted of Yahweh's "life" or "blessing", and was believed to be the source of the welfare, peace and prosperity of his people. When therefore we inquire about the meaning and efficacy of cultic acts we must look for both in the conception of Yahweh's presence which the cult presupposed. This provided the context of religious ideas and symbolism in which every ritual

---

7 This should probably be dated *c.* 1200 B.C.

act took place, and defined the source of blessing which the cult made available. The worshipper's attention was directed to the God of the sanctuary to which the gift was brought, rather than to the potency of his act of offering. Thus, although ritual acts had a symbolic character, and often originated in a religious milieu which asserted a more direct bond between God and nature than was later accepted in Israel, this symbolic element was not given the greatest prominence. Interest was drawn not to the act itself, but to the presence of the deity before whom the act was performed.

The conception of the cultic presence of God was no mere metaphor, or archaic survival from an earlier age, but the fundamental basis upon which all of Israel's worship was built.[8] Thus the basic expression for visiting a sanctuary was "to go up to see the face of God".[9] This expression certainly derived from pre-Israelite times, and from a form of worship in which divine images were employed,[10] but it continued in use in Israel as a fundamental expression of the meaning and purpose of worship. Thus even though the various festivals, rituals, and types of sacrifice which were performed in Israel were largely adopted from earlier cults, and did not emerge *de novo* in Israel, they assumed a new character when they were employed in the service of Israel's God. They became part of the service of Yarweh, and ceased consciously to be connected with the other gods to which they had once belonged. In this way the distinctive features of Israel's religion gradually permeated the rites and symbols of its worship, and invested them with a meaning which was uniquely Israelite. This was a development which was spread over a long period, and was not the action of any one group, or of any movement, although certain occasions and movements, especially the Deuteronomic, were particularly influential. The fact that a particular ritual act had a pre-Israelite history and origin, therefore, does not necessarily tell us a great

---

[8] Cf. for further elaboration of this my book *God and Temple. The Idea of the Divine Presence in Ancient Israel*, Oxford, 1965.

[9] Ex. 23. 17; 34. 23; Ps. 42. 3 (Evv. 2) etc. Later generations of Jews interpreted the active "see" as a reflexive "to appear before". On the history of this expression see W. W. von Baudissin, " 'Gott schauen' " in der alttestamentlichen Religion", *Archiv für Religionswissenschaft* 18, 1915, pp. 173-239, and F. Nötscher, *"Das Angesicht Gottes schauen" nach biblischer und babylonischer Auffassung*, Würzburg, 1924.

[10] W. W. von Baudissin, op. cit., pp. 189ff.; F. Nötscher, op. cit., pp. 89ff.

deal about the way in which such an act was interpreted in Israel, since is was adopted into a different environment.[11] Similar acts could therefore have quite different meanings within different religious traditions, and there can be little doubt that even within the boundaries of Israel's religion different local traditions vested similar acts with varying interpretations. The need for providing a unified and authoritative interpretation of the cult was a very real one during the Old Testament period, and this is clearly evidenced in the various strata of the Pentateuch.

In recent study two particular aspects of Israel's worship have received considerable attention, and each of them enables us to see something of the meaning of worship in its total context. The first of these aspects is what we may briefly term the function of worship in society. Particular rites and festivals were observed in affirmation of the sanctity and authority of certain social and political institutions. In Israel this has received most attention in regard to the Autumn Festival, which has been claimed to have possessed at one time the character of a covenant festival, affirming the divine institution of the Israelite amphictyony of tribes.[12] The uniquely Israelite character of this celebration was derived from the fact that it was the primary bond of unity in the political structure of the tribal federation which constituted Israel. This aspect of the meaning of worship in early Israel has been well argued by H. J. Kraus,[13] but it is also strongly evident in A. Weiser's interpretation of the Psalms.[14] Weiser regards this covenant festival as the fundamental institution of Israel, recalling and reaffirming the Sinai covenant, and giving rise to the tradition upon which the Pentateuch grew up. Other scholars have also regarded this social and political function of worship as investing Israel's sacrifices with a distinctive meaning which they did not afterwards lose. Thus even when the amphictyonic political structure had disappeared, the religious meaning of Israel's covenant with Yahweh could still be regarded as finding primary expression through the offering of particular

---

11 Cf. C. Westermann, "Sinn und Grenze religionsgeschichtliche Parallelen", *ThLZ* 90, 1965, cols. 489-96.

12 Cf. M. Noth, *Das System der Zwölf Stämme Israels*, (BWANT IV: 1), Stuttgart, 1930, pp. 66ff.

13 H. J. Kraus, *Worship in Israel. A Cultic History of the Old Testament*, Oxford, 1966, esp. pp. 125ff.

14 A. Weiser, *The Psalms*, London, 1962, *passim.*

sacrifices.[15] Certainly this is one aspect of the meaning of worship in Israel which becomes apparent in a consideration of the social context in which the cult was celebrated. It must not be limited solely to a connexion with the Sinai covenant, however, since the Psalter shows clearly that the liturgy of the Jerusalem temple was deeply influenced by the belief in the divine election of the Davidic monarchy. Such worship not only derived support from the Davidic monarchy, but was itself intended to point to the divine authority which the latter possessed.[16]

This social function of worship in Israel must be allied with another aspect of its meaning which modern scholarship has sought to illuminate. This is its concern with Israel's history, and especially with its "actualizing" of past events through their recollection and dramatic re-presentation in the cult.[17] This actualization of the past must be closely related to the social and political function of worship, because the events which were so dramatically recalled in the cult were those which proclaimed the divine election on which Israel's existence rested. Thus we find that the Feast of Passover particularly recalled the event of the exodus from Egypt,[18] and this process of linking particular festivals with specific historical events was continued and developed in later Judaism. Thus history rather than myth came to provide the sacred *logos* of Israelite worship. The nature of this actualizing of historical events in the cult has been variously interpreted, and has sometimes been given an extreme emphasis, but when set within the context of the belief in the cultic presence of God its character becomes clear. Israel encountered in its worship the presence of the God who had dealt graciously with it in the past, and the recollection of this providential history served to define his nature and character, and to remind his worshippers of their debt to him. The cultic celebration

---

[15] Cf. A. Arens, *Die Psalmen im Gottesdienst des Alten Bundes*, Trier, 1959, pp. 111ff., and R. Schmid, *Das Bundesopfer in Israel. Wesen, Ursprung, und Bedeutung der alttestamentlichen Schelamim*, (Studien zum Alten und Neuen Testament IX), Munich, pp. 101ff.

[16] H. J. Kraus, op. cit., pp. 179ff.

[17] Cf. especially, A. Weiser, *The Psalms, passim*; H. Zirker, *Die kultische Vergegenwärtigung der Vergangenheit in den Psalmen*, (Bonner biblische Beiträge 20), Bonn, 1964; C. Westermann, "Vergegenwärtigung der Geschichte in den Psalmen", *Forschung am Alten Testament, Gesammelte Studien*, (Theologische Bücherei 24), Munich, 1964, pp. 306-35.

[18] Ex. 23. 15; Deut. 16. 4-8.

was a bridge between the present and the past, because in the cult the God who had delivered Israel in the past was present and active. We cannot therefore evaluate the character of this actualization of the past without relating it to the conception of the presence of God in his sanctuary when men gathered to worship him. Thus when we seek for the meaning of Israel's cult we find that this is illuminated both by a consideration of the social organization which such cultic acts upheld, and by the distinctive concern with history which was introduced into them. It would be wrong, however, to define the meaning of Israelite worship solely in terms of its social function, or its historical concern. Viewed in retrospect, one of the remarkable features of Israel's worship was that it never ceased to retain immense significance and value for individuals, in spite of great political changes, and through historical events of tragic proportions. Israel's worship was never anchored to one political structure so exclusively that it could not survive when this form passed away. In this respect it was very dissimilar from the religions of its neighbours. The reason for this persistence of Israel's worship lies in the distinctive character of the religious ideas which it upheld, and its continuing power to mediate a sense of the presence of God.

3. THE THEOLOGICAL SIGNIFICANCE OF ISRAEL'S WORSHIP

We have argued above that the meaning of cultic acts in Israel must not be looked for primarily in the individual symbolism which they undoubtedly possessed, but in the whole context of worship in which they were celebrated. The original significance of a rite, and the interpretation of its symbolism, were not always consciously apprehended by worshippers, or were at best only imperfectly known. This is suggested by the fact that neither the psalms which accompanied such acts, nor the written traditions which were preserved as an authority for their continued use, clearly defined this symbolism or explained its origin. Rather the context of worship lent meaning to individual ritual acts, and encouraged belief in their efficacy.

We have preserved in the written traditions of the Old Testament the literary deposit of two major attempts to provide a comprehensive interpretation of Israel's cult. These may broadly be classed as the Deuteronomic and the Priestly traditions, both of which provided an authoritative presentation of the significance of the Jerusalem cultus.[19] Each represents the outcome of a movement which was influential over a long period, and each undoubtedly included in its range ideas and institutions of great antiquity. The Deuteronomic is the earlier of these movements, and its written law code became an important factor in the reformation of the Jerusalem temple worship in Josiah's reign. In the Book of Deuteronomy we find that certain theological and moral ideas are set in the forefront of the interpretation of worship, and a whole range of civil and cultic matters are brought together in an integrated theological system. The ideas which the cult upheld became even more important than the individual actions of which it was composed. Most noticeable is that the idea of the cultic presence of Yahweh is given a theological interpretation in terms of Yahweh's sending forth his name to dwell at the sanctuary.[20] Thus a theological idea is used as an explanation of the traditional symbolism of the sanctuary which asserted the divine presence there. Similarly the various types of sacrifice are interpreted by the Deuteronomists as gifts to God,[21] expressing the worshipper's gratitude for God's abundant gifts, supremely exemplified in his gift of the land. Any suggestion that a physical relationship existed between the sacrificial victim and God, or that it satisfied a particular need on the part of God, is rejected, and its significance is found in its expression of the moral and spiritual qualities of human gratitude. The meaning of worship lies in its significance for men, and in its ability to express their response to God. Any suggestion that it supplied some felt need of God is firmly repudiated, as it is also in Psalm 50. In this way we can see that the interpretation of sacrifice became all important since its value as a rite lay in the attitude of the offerer

---

[19] The reasons for connecting Deuteronomy with Jerusalem as the sanctuary of Yahweh's choice are set out in my article "Deuteronomy and the Jerusalem Cult Tradition", *VT* 15, 1965, pp. 300-12.

[20] Deut. 12. 5, 11, 21; 14. 23f.; 16. 2, 6, 11; cf. 1 Kings 8. 15-21. On this doctrine see especially G. von Rad, *Studies in Deuteronomy*, (SBT 9), London, 1953, pp. 37ff. and *Old Testament Theology*, Vol. 1, Edinburgh, 1962, p. 238.

[21] Deut. 12. 10ff.; 14. 22ff.; 16. 16f. Cf. G. B. Gray, *Sacrifice in the Old Testament. Its Theory and Practice*, Oxford, 1925, pp. 45ff., especially p. 47, "Thus, though in Deuteronomy the belief that sacrifices are gifts to God is certainly not discarded, sacrifice is less regarded as a means to obtain God's favour than as an opportunity for acknowledging his goodness and the manifold benefits which he has bestowed".

which it expressed. Its efficacy was related to the spiritual relationship which existed between the offerer and God, rather than in any mysterious power with which the sacrificial victim was charged, or in its ability to satisfy a divine need.

In the Deuteronomistic History, which shows an attitude to the cult which has a close relationship to that of Deuteronomy, we find a similar emphasis upon the spiritual and personal meaning of worship in the Prayer for the Dedication of the Temple (1 Kings 8. 14-53). This is undoubtedly a composition from the Deuteronomistic Historian himself. In all the ways in which it is envisaged that God will intervene through worship on behalf of his people it is particularly stressed that communion with God is established through prayer, and the ritual acts performed in the temple find their meaning through this. Thus once again the attitude of the worshipper, and his appreciation of what is taking place become vital to the efficacy of the ritual acts which are enacted in the temple.

This emphasis in Deuteronomy and the Deuteronomistic History upon the element of meaning attaching to the cult, and the need for an appreciation of this meaning by the worshipper is found elsewhere in the Old Testament, and there can be little doubt that it represents a development which had its origins in the cult itself. Its appearance in Deuteronomy may well have been greatly encouraged by the criticisms of Israel's cult made by the eighth century prophets, but even before this we know that the use of psalms and liturgies as an accompaniment to sacrificial acts introduced into the cult an element of interpretation and personal application.[22]

In the Priestly Document we find an importance attached to the meaning of cultic acts which bears close comparison with that of Deuteronomy, although there are many differences of detail. Not only are individual ritual acts shown to have a particular meaning, but all such acts are incorporated into a comprehensive theological system.[23] In both the Deuteronomic and Priestly movements we see evidence that there took place in Israel a development in which the

[22] Cf. S. Mowinckel, *The Psalms in Israel's Worship*, Oxford, 1962, Vol. I, pp. 20ff; *Religion und Kultus*, pp. 117ff.
[23] Cf. G. von Rad, *Old Testament Theology*, Vol. I, pp. 241ff; M. Haran, "The Complex of Ritual Acts Performed inside the Tabernacle", *Scripta Hierosolymitana VIII*, 1961, pp. 272ff.

cult was theologized and spiritualized, and this process was of immense significance for the rise of Judaism, and for the appearance of an Old Testament canon of sacred scriptures. One of the major influences which contributed to the emergence of authoritative canonical writings was the need for providing the worship of the temple that was rebuilt in Jerusalem after the exile with an authoritative interpretation, and for making clear the distinctive traditions which it upheld.

The development of spiritualization in Israel's worship has been given a careful investigation by H. J. Hermisson,[24] who argues that this development took place over almost the entire period of Israel's cultic history, and derives initially from tendencies which entered Israel in Solomon's reign, in the international atmosphere of the Jerusalem royal court. In this process external cultic rites were so closely bound to the moral and spiritual attitude of the worshipper that the act became the sign and symbol of the latter. There is no doubt that during the Old Testament period the emphasis upon the meaning of cultic acts was so strongly pressed as to show that an awareness of this meaning by the worshipper was believed to be vital to the efficacy of the act. There was therefore a distinction between the objective cultic act and its subjective meaning for the worshipper.

It is important to make clear exactly what we mean by spiritualization. This can be taken as a description of that process which we observe in the Old Testament by which the external rites of worship were given a theological meaning and an individual application in terms of the personal communion of the worshipper with God. It is, however, usually taken to mean more than this and to point to that development by which the subjective attitude of the worshipper, and his expression of this in moral conduct, were considered to be equivalent, or superior, to the actual performance of cultic rites. In this way the cult was translated into terms of a subjective spiritual communion with God which no longer needed the support of external visible rites. There is no doubt that this

---

[24] H. J. Hermisson, *Sprache und Ritus im altisraelitischen Kult. Zur "Spiritualisierung" der Kultbegriffe im Alten Testament* (WMANT 19), Neukirchen—Vluyn, 1965. Later evidence is collected in H. Wenschkewitz, *Die Spiritualisierung der Kultbegriffe Tempel, Priester, und Opfer im Neuen Testament*, Angelos, Beih. 4, 1932.

type of non-cultic piety did develop in Judaism, and was materially advanced by the destruction of the Jerusalem temple in A.D. 70. This radical spiritualization of the cult, however, is not truly evidenced in the Old Testament, where the emphasis upon the spiritual meaning of cultic acts is not intended to dispense with these acts themselves.

We find in the Old Testament a deepening emphasis upon the subjective meaning of cultic acts, and a strong awareness of the personal nature of communion with God by which his blessing is apprehended, without any clear evidence that a total spiritualization has taken place. Cultic acts are accepted as valid means for establishing communion between God and man, but their efficacy is closely related to the personal and spiritual apprehension of their meaning by the worshipper. Israel did not accept the complete unity of outward act and inward meaning, but took very careful measures to ensure that the worshipper appreciated the true significance of what he was doing. The saying in the Book of Proverbs is undoubtedly representative of a deep-rooted attitude in Judaism : "The sacrifice of the wicked is an abomination; how much more when he brings it with evil intent" (Prov. 21. 27; cf. 15. 8).

If the worshipper did not understand the meaning of his action, and adopt an attitude consonant with it, then his offering was to no purpose.

This interpretation is further testified in the Wisdom of Ben Sira,[25] and is further elaborated in the writings of post-biblical Judaism.[26] In a famous passage in the Mishnah tractate Yoma (8. 8ff.) the offering of a guilt offering without repentance is declared void. H. H. Rowley sums up the weight of evidence, "Where sacrifice was prescribed and offered, it must be the organ of the spirit of the offerer before it could be the organ of the power of God unto him or on his behalf." [27] There is no doubt therefore that Judaism did

---

25 Ecclus. 34. 18ff.
26 Cf. J. Behm, *Theological Dictionary of the New Testament*, ed. G. Kittel, Vol. III, Grand Rapids, 1966, pp. 186ff; G. F. Moore, *Judaism in the First Centuries of the Christian Era. The Age of the Tannaim,* Harvard, 1927, Vol. I, pp. 498ff, 504ff, Vol. II, pp. 14f.
27 H. H. Rowley, "The Meaning of Sacrifice in the Old Testament", *From Moses to Qumran,* London, 1963, pp. 99f. Cf. also G. F. Moore, op. cit., Vol. I, p. 505, "The important thing is that while the temple was still standing the principle had been established that the efficacy of every species of expiation was morally conditioned—without repentance no rites availed".

make a clear distinction between outward act and inward meaning, which was the outcome of a profound attempt to show the theological significance of the cult. The roots of such a theological and spiritual movement lie far back in the Old Testament period. When historical circumstances compelled it, by the destruction of the Jerusalem temple, this movement was carried still further by the substitution of cultic attitudes for cultic acts. For the Old Testament word and rite belonged together, and the outward act required to be interpreted and understood before the worshipper could make it the vehicle of his own communion with God. Both as to the conduct of the cult, and the teaching regarding its efficacy, Judaism did make a clear distinction between the outward performance of a rite, and its inner value for the devout worshipper. In doing so it did not reject the cult, but regarded it as God's appointed gift to Israel, and sought to ensure that it expressed the true spiritual nature of his communion with his people.

2

THE EUCHARIST
IN I CORINTHIANS

AUSTIN FARRER

Dr G. D. Kilpatrick delivered two discourses at the University of Geneva in 1964, and published the substance of them in the *Revue de théologie et de philosophie* for the same year, under the title, "The Eucharist in the New Testament". I propose to discuss that article, both because it deserves serious consideration, and because the discussion of it opens a ready way into the heart of a vital question. I shall not presume an acquaintance on my readers' part with Dr Kilpatrick's French text; I shall state his views and arguments before I comment on them. But before I do either the one or the other, I will put the gist of his contentions into the fewest possible words.

He raises the question how the traditional narrative of Christ's sacramental institution was related in New Testament times to the celebration of the Supper. He concludes that the narrative functioned as a customary recitation declaring the origin and the significance of the rite, together with the authority prescribing and the rules governing its performance. The narrative did not serve as a consecrating formula. He then asks what it was that did effect a consecration of the sacramental elements; and his answer is, the sacrificial character of the rite. Let me say at once that with these two conclusions, thus barely stated, I find myself in agreement. There are, however, subsidiary questions of no small interest, on which I have answers to propose alternative to Dr Kilpatrick's. I will mention two, one arising out of each of his main positions. *i*. How was the recitation used? Was it a feature of the sacramental ceremony or was it a piece of catechism learnt by heart and intended to be borne in mind? Dr Kilpatrick inclines to the former and I to the latter opinion. *ii.* What phase or element of the sacrificial action was seen as consecratory? Dr Kilpatrick thinks the worshippers' offering of the gifts; I think, the Deity's reception of them.

Before turning to Dr Kilpatrick's arguments, I wish to narrow the subject under discussion in point of time. Dr Kilpatrick's title is "The Eucharist in the New Testament". But did either eucharistic practice or eucharistic doctrine remain fixed, in a period at once so extended and so formative as that covered by the composition of the Canonical Writings? It is more convenient to take a single phase. In fact, Dr Kilpatrick centres his discussion on St Paul's First Epistle to Corinth; and I have worded the title of this essay accordingly. Other writings will, of course, cast light on the Pauline position; but it is this alone that we shall endeavour to clarify.

Dr Kilpatrick starts from a broad and manifestly relevant background of analogy. Sacred texts were recited at sacrificial ceremonies in the ancient world, as the *Myth and Ritual* school of writers have reminded us. The recitation did not produce the sacrificial effect; it narrated a story of institution, giving the worshippers the ground for belief that what they did would be efficacious; and perhaps reminding the Deity that he was in some way pledged to find their sacrifice acceptable. To the first-century Israelite, such recitations were no mere features of an age-old heathendom. Rabbinic evidence leaves us in no doubt that in the latter years of the Second Temple the High Priest read out the Mosaic institution of Atonement Sacrifice while his subordinates burned the beasts on the Great Day (Mishna, Yoma, vii. l); or that a liturgy of question and answer within the bosom of the Jewish family drew out an account of the Paschal institution on the night when the Passover was eaten (Ibid., Pesahim 10. 4).

The psychology underlying such customs scarcely needs interpretation; and there is no mystery of motive to explain, when we see the Church in due course moved to incorporate the narrative of the Last Supper in her eucharistic rite. Indeed, one can strengthen the point—the Church had uniquely powerful motives for so doing, motives implicit in the special character of her faith. The Christians could do nothing but by implementation of Christ's action. The Jewish priests knew how to make an acceptable atonement with the only true sacrificial blood available under the Old Covenant. The Christians could claim no such ability. Christ alone had offered or could offer true atoning blood. His disciples merely set forth bread and wine, and without reliance on Christ's institution to establish the equivalence of their bread and wine with his body and blood, they could not suppose themselves to be doing anything. A careless Israelite might accept Atonement Day as a ritual spring-cleaning, efficacious in itself, and forget whether it had been instituted by Moses or by Melchizedek. A similar attitude on the part of a Christian communicant is scarcely conceivable.

The special consideration we have just offered has a curiously two-sided effect on Dr Kilpatrick's line of argument. On the one hand it strengthens the attachment of the Christian rites to their *Myth and Ritual* background; on the other hand it weakens the consequence he wishes to found on that attachment. The institution-narrative was extraneous to sacrificial efficacy under the Old Covenant, because it was not Aaron, but the High Priest of the day, who made the sacrifice. The celebrant of the Christian Eucharist can achieve the purposes of the rite "in Christ" alone; and so it cannot be in every sense denied that the memorial of Christ's act enters into that consecration of the sacramental elements which the celebrant effects. What can be denied is that the narrative served the primitive celebrant as a consecrating formula. Perhaps he consecrated by simply doing what the Lord had done.

Is anything inevitable in the history of rites? If anything is, we may reckon it to have been inevitable that the Church should come to incorporate the Institution-Narrative in her eucharistic liturgy. But how soon? No one doubts that the Atonement ceremonies were performed for generations before Leviticus was read over them, and the Passover for centuries before father and son did their parson-and-clerk responses at dinner. Had the Narrative already established its place in the eucharistic ceremonies at Corinth, say twenty-five years after the Institution it narrated? If we are to form a probable opinion, we have two fields we must explore: the ritual conditions obtaining, and the suggestions carried by the text of the Narrative (1 Cor. 11. 23-25).

Dr Kilpatrick does not discuss the ritual conditions at Corinth; and one can well understand that so conscientious a scholar should hesitate to open a field of inquiry too wide for adequate treatment within the scope of his essay. Yet it is impossible to judge the question he has in hand without forming an opinion on the subject; and so we will state our belief, however imperfectly grounded.

What did go on at Corinth? The disorders rebuked by St Paul are unintelligible without the supposition that the community united on the Lord's Day to eat the meal of the day together; and St Paul's direction is for them to go on doing so, only in good order. Let them wait for all to arrive before they begin; let them share their provisions round. If they want to have eating and drinking parties (for themselves and their intimates), they should do it at home. This last piece of advice has been built up by rash interpreters into an apostolic direction to take all serious eating out of the sacred feast. But so radical a proposal could never have been made so casually.

It has been too readily assumed that the careless behaviour of the Corinthians should be explained by the survival in minds converted from heathendom of pagan attitudes to nominally religious feasts. In fact, Jewish habits of mind will explain the matter just as well. The first tractate of the Mishna, Berakhoth 7. 4, 5, shows us the rabbis deciding when orthodox Jewish feasters may, and when they may not, separate into parties, each party saying grace for itself. Whatever licence the rabbis allowed, and however tolerable in a Jewish community, separation must make it impossible, as St Paul says, to eat a Lord's Supper. One grace must be said for bread, and one for wine, with accompanying distributions from the one broken loaf and the one cup of blessing. And where the graces are one, the feasting and drinking must be one, taking their time from the graces. The Corinthians may simply be treating the Eucharist as what it is in form, a Jewish community-meal; St Paul insisting on what it is in substance, a holy sacrifice.

The ancients normally drank after they had eaten, and St Paul tells us that Christ said the grace for wine in the common place, "after they had supped". The burden of proof lies with the interpreter who would maintain that St Paul expected his Corinthians to do otherwise. And so we have no right to suppose any single great eucharistic prayer in which a narrative of Christ's institution might conveniently have found a place. All we can fairly assume is two little ceremonies, performed while hungry and thirsty people kept their hands off their provisions; the only spoken part of either ceremony being a thanksgiving for meat or for drink. It was indeed a Jewish custom to expand the common graces with extra clauses on special occasions, especially the grace over the cup. But how far would that go? Whatever we think of that enigmatic treatise, *The Teaching of the Twelve Apostles*, it may be fairly taken to exhibit primtive models for Christianizations of the table-blessings; and they are not of anything like the sort of scope which would make the inclusion of the Narrative credible. In any case, the Narrative as it stands is a single story, not divisible into two self-contained parts. How could it be fitted to separate graces for bread and for wine?

It is difficult to believe that anyone who accepts the sort of picture I have drawn will suppose the Christians to have worked the Institution-Narrative into their rites under such conditions. They could hardly think of doing so before two radical changes had taken place, changes which no modern historian can date within decades: the taking of the sacramental acts out of the evening meal, to become a sequel upon the Church's equivalent for morning synagogue; and the combination of the two graces into one continuous eucharistic prayer, preceding and hallowing both acts of communion. Such a prayer, indeed, was fitted to accommodate a narrative recording the double institution of loaf and of cup.

Though the holy supper implied by St Paul's admonitions looks an unlikely setting for a recital of the Narrative, perhaps those admonitions nevertheless suggest that the recital took place. Do they? I do not think so. The Apostle's converts are doing violence to the sacrament, as though they had forgotten its vital attachment to the Last Supper. He reminds them of the tradition he had given them on the subject; and it is surely more natural to suppose them forgetful of their catechism than deaf to their liturgy; all the more so, in view of the close formal parallel between 1 Corinthians 11. 23 and 15. 3. The Corinthians misuse the Supper; have they forgotten the tradition St Paul handed on to them as he had received it—how that the Lord Jesus, in the night on which he was bertayed . . . ? The Corinthians misbelieve the resurrection; have they then forgotten the tradition St Paul handed on to them as he had received it—how that Christ died for our sins according to the scriptures . . . ? If the tradition of chapter 15 is catechism rather than liturgy, why should the tradition of chapter 11 be liturgy, rather than catechism?

So far we have found little to favour belief in the liturgical use of the Institution-Narrative in St Paul's churches. But then we have not

yet heard Dr Kilpatrick's contentions. They amount to the claim
that the Narrative itself bears every mark of being a liturgical piece.
They fall under three heads, and I shall state each in argumentative
form, even at the risk of doing some violence to the scholarly
moderation of an author who prefers to let his observations carry
their own weight. For without formalizing his contentions into
arguments, I do not see how I am to bring them to the bar of judgement. A further liberty I will take is of altering the order in which
they are presented.

1. The Pauline Institution-Narrative reads like a piece of liturgy,
well-rubbed in use. The point can be brought out by a comparison of
the Pauline version with the nearest-contemporary Gospel form, the
Marcan. We shall find ourselves led to judge that of the two the
Pauline is the more primitive in substance, but the more developed
in Greek style. Indeed it exhibits hellenizations which we should
not ascribe to St Paul himself, since he is very capable of letting
semitisms stand, when he is traversing Semitic ground. We should
suppose therefore that the text before us in his Epistle was already
shaped before he received it, by speakers more uncompromisingly
Hellenistic than himself; the leaders (say) of the church at Antioch.
And how would it have been so shaped by them, except in liturgical
use?

What are we to say to this argument? First, that the comparison
drawn between St Mark and St Paul carries all the authority of its
author's scholarship. Second, that the arguments he bases upon it
involve the following assumptions.

a. That St Paul, if he had worded the Institution for himself, would
have wished to leave to it its biblical-sounding Semitic overtones,
rather than to give it that current Greek idiom which he was
capable of writing when he chose.

b. That the Greeks at Antioch must be supposed to have made their
original translation of the Aramaic narrative with semitizing
literalness, rather than to have phrased an equivalent story in a
more current Greek, straight away.

c. That repetition in liturgical use could have led to the helleni-
zation, whereas repetition in catechetical use could not. I confess

that I cannot place much reliance on any of these assumptions and especially not on the last.

2. St Paul's Institution-Narrative is no general account of Christ's last supper with his friends; it is a rigidly limited selection of what bears upon the celebration of the Eucharist. Everything it contains, indeed, serves either as model or as prescription for something actually done in the primitive ecclesia, unless we must except Christ's declaratory words, "This is my body . . . This is the new covenant in my blood . . . " But it is unnecessary to allow the exception, if the declaratory words themselves were repeated in the rite. Now there is no evidence of their ever having been so repeated, except as part and parcel of the Institution-Narrative. It is natural, then, to suppose that they were always included, and always in their narrative setting.

Once again, the argument rests on assumption. The assumption here concerns the principle governing the selection of material to stand in the Narrative. Everything selected should serve as model or prescription for what was to be done. But why should we assume this selective principle, rather than a more elastic criterion—the criterion of vital relevance to what should be done? We have no irrelevances, even on the hypothesis that the Narrative was not liturgically recited: nothing but prescription for what should be done, or declaration of that divine meaning which alone made it worth the doing. I cannot see why a narrative formula taught as catechism should not be happily compounded of these two elements.

3. The Narrative contains a virtual invitation to recite it at the Supper. It lies in the words, "Do this for my memorial" (εἰς τὴν ἐμὴν ἀνάμνησιν). The phrase should be taken to mean "In commemoration of my redemptive act", the very act epitomized in the Narrative. How better, then, should they make the commemoration, than by reciting the Narrative?

The argument rests on two positions; Dr Kilpatrick's gloss upon "Do this for my memorial"; and his assumption that "a memorial of Christ's redemptive act" would naturally include a recitation of the Institution. Christ's redemptive act was his death and resurrection. The Institution-Narrative shows how that act was and can be sacramentally realized. It is scarcely evident that a sacramental memorial of the redemptive act should memorialize the institution of that memorial.

To turn now to Dr Kilpatrick's gloss. To establish it, he reviews the interpretations which have been or can be put upon the Lord's words. His review is most interesting on its own account, and quite apart from the place it holds in his general argument. I shall continue to set the matter out in my own way, while endeavouring to miss none of his points. First, then, there is no ambiguity about the grammatical sense. "For my memorial" means "to awaken a memory *of me*" and not anything like "to awaken *my* memory (of you)". Second, it would be natural to suppose that the Speaker had in mind the identity of the person or persons in whom a memory of him was to be awakened. It might be, as has commonly been thought, his disciples themselves; but then again, as Dr Jeremias has so forcibly suggested, it might be the Divine Father. Old Testament usage can be quoted in Dr Jeremias's support; Jewry was familiar with the dramatic figure, according to which a man's offering might be seen as a memorial before God, pressing upon him the claims of the offerer. Is not the Divine Father to be reminded of his Son, until he sees fit to establish his kingdom?

Dr Kilpatrick rejects the suggestion, on the ground that it is false to the context. Jesus is dwelling among present facts—the Body going to its death, the Blood ready to be spilt—and we ought not, without evidence, to switch the reference of his concluding phrases to a plea for Advent. The objection is not, however, conclusive. It was a familiar idea that a martyr's blood, like Abel's, cried from the ground for vindication; to remind God, therefore, of the blood-shedding was to remind him that he was pledged to dethrone murder and to crown righteousness. According to Matthew 23. 29-36, Christ's passion fills up the measure of all the Abel-blood shed since the foundation of the world, and assures the Great Vindication within the days of Caiaphas's generation. According to Revelation 6. 6-11, the measure will be made full by the association of the Christian martyrs with the Slaughtered Lamb; their souls, run down in blood under God's altar, cry for early vindication, and the sacrificial liturgy of heaven presents their "memorial" before God. Dr Jeremias's suggestion retains its force.

If we set it aside, and take the awakened memory to be that of the communicants, our difficulty is to put any gloss upon the phrase which will accord with anything St Paul or his friends could have seen themselves as doing. In a profane context men might hold a commemorative feast at a friend's tomb, and describe the meal as "his memorial"; but as Dr Kilpatrick very justly says, the Christians did not think they had been willed to do anything like that. The phrase must somehow be loaded with theology. His own solution is to cite the recalling, or making mention, of the mighty acts of the Lord which characterized Old Testament religion, and which remained an integral part of synagogue worship on the side of praise and thanksgiving. The Christian Eucharist obtains its very name from the thanksgivings it contains. Why should not the memorial of Christ which Christ had commanded have been understood as a thanksgiving for the divine work accomplished in him?

Nothing might seem more reasonable; only it is necessary to go a little further. The thanksgiving both in Israel's worship and in the Church's Eucharist was directed to God the Father. The "memorial", as Dr Kilpatrick would have it, should therefore be a grateful setting forth before the Father of the Son's redemptive death. But if so, then Dr Kilpatrick's disagreement with Dr Jeremias is not very desperate. Who can prevent the pledge of mercies still to come from mixing in men's thoughts with the substance of mercies already received, or pleas for fulfilment with thanks for achievement? In fact, we should suppose it to be the other way about—the pleading for fulfilment came first, being more consonant with Christ's situation at the Supper; the sense of the blessings attaching to the Christians' present standing in Christ had its place in the experience of the Church.

We said above that Jesus would naturally be thought to have had in mind the identity of the person or persons in whom a recollection of him was to be aroused. There is nevertheless a line of interpretation still to be considered which leaves that issue open. It has been claimed by liturgiologists that "anamnesis", in liturgical contexts, carries an objective or realistic sense. The matters recalled are not so much brought into anyone's recollection as in some way made present in virtue and in power.

Dr Kilpatrick objects that it was the development of the Christian liturgy itself which loaded anamnesis with all this meaning; there is no evidence of so mystical a value for the word, either in the New Testament or in its linguistic background. To adduce "the liturgical sense of anamnesis" by way of explanation for Christ's words is, therefore, simply to put the cart before the horse. Dr Kilpatrick is certainly right; but what he says does not amount to a disproof of any claim that the liturgical anamnesis was already in New Testament times acquiring the "liturgical sense". If the Lord and his death were set forth with all the realism of sacramental presence for "a memorial before God" and for thankful remembrance to God, it was natural for men's thoughts to centre on a presentation (to be felt in heaven and on earth), rather than on anyone's remembering.

There were ideas in the field which might favour such developments. The Name of the Lord, mentioned or recalled with due solemnity, manifested a present power; and so in rabbinic thought the Name was associated with the Spirit. Now there is evidence too familiar to need quotation, for the extension of such ideas from the Name of the Lord JHVH to the Name of the Lord Jesus. May we not say, then, that to make a memorial of Jesus was anyhow to recall his Name, and that to recall it by a sacramental rite was to recall it with the greatest solemnity? The Name was more effectually present through actions than through words alone, as Jesus had implied in his own teaching about the irremissible sin, blasphemy (of the Name). When evil spirits are expelled in the Name of God (and how else could they be honestly expelled?) the Name is so visibly present in power of Spirit, that to call the exorcism Satanic is to incur the guilt of blasphemy (Mark 30. 28-30).

To conclude: the several views which Dr Kilpatrick contrasts are not so much opposed, perhaps, as complementary. We cannot deny him his gloss on "anamnesis", though we are far from allowing it exclusive right. It may well be that by the time St Paul was writing to Corinth Christian communicants indeed felt themselves to be making in the sight of God a thankful memorial of their Redeemer. If he is free to suppose so, Dr Kilpatrick thinks he will have additional reason to see the Pauline celebrant as expatiating on thanks for redemption in his prayer of grace, and if on redemption, then on the Narrative of the Last Supper. But even conceding Dr Kilpatrick his gloss, the corollary he makes it carry is not strong. The Christians might find their grateful commemoration of redeeming work in doing what Christ had commanded, whatever the celebrant did or did not pack into his prayer of grace.

Dr Kilpatrick has an additional argument, which I will not number with the rest, since it is admittedly extraneous. If, he says, the Institution-Narrative was in liturgical use, it would make it easy for St John to expound in chapter 6 of his gospel a history he nowhere records. But first, St John was writing, we may well suppose, a good forty years after St Paul, when liturgical usage might well have developed; and second, St John (surely) makes no *historical* allusion such as to mystify any communicant who had ever been told what the sacrament was.

So much for our examination of the first part of Dr Kilpatrick's essay. We turn to the second, and we are happy to see that our disagreement with him over the liturgical use of the Institution-Narrative in no way obstructs our following him in his next step. If, he says, the place of the Narrative was in the thanksgiving, rather than in any consecratory formula, it remains to be asked what was felt to effect a consecration. It does indeed, and no less so if the Narrative was absent from the liturgy altogether.

He first considers the view that the grace-before-meat itself consecrated. Not, of course, that the Israelite blessed his food; he blessed the Giver of it. Yet the blessing of God was held to make his gifts proper for human use. The mere fact that it was unfit to use them without first blessing him, meant that to bless him made them fit. A more thoughtful mind might reflect that what the Giver could be sincerely thanked for, might be taken to be enjoyed with his goodwill. No good thing was to be rejected that could be received with thanksgiving (1 Tim. 4. 4, 5; cf. 1 Cor. 10. 30).

So the grace hallowed the table. But, as Dr Kilpatrick acutely observes, such hallowing fell far short of what St Paul's words imply. It was scarcely more than negative—the removal of any obstacle to the free use of God's gifts. It was not positive, it did not charge them with supernatural sanctity, such sanctity as to account for St Paul's declaration that to misuse the Communion is sacrilege, liable to be visited with sickness or with death.

Of course St Paul does not say that the misuse is a ritual or physical transgression; but that does not mean that the sanctity is not inherent. Since, he tells us, Christ had declared the bread his body, and the cup a new covenant in his blood, *therefore* to taste the bread and the cup in a manner that is unworthy of them is to be guilty of sin against the body and blood of the Lord, and to invite physical judgements. They are worthily partaken when they are allowed their proper effect of sanctifying a genuine eating-and-drinking-together of the whole community in the Spirit of Christ. When they are not allowed this their proper effect, they are partaken of unworthily.

It is true as far as it goes that the sin denounced is an offence against the brethren; but that is not the whole story, for who can believe that St Paul would threaten with divine judgements of sickness and death thoughtless misbehaviour at dinner? It is misbehaviour in a special context, evidently; and St Paul defines that context not (for example) as a solemn gathering of the Holy Church in the Name of the Lord, but as a partaking of the body and blood in such a way as either to honour or to dishonour them.[1] We moderns can ask, if we wish, whether the offence is sacrilege or uncharity, but we can be certain that the alternatives we pose were no alternatives for St Paul. It is like that other notorious modern question, whether faith or baptism makes a Christian. St Paul spiritualizes the sacraments; he does not spiritualize them away.

We must grant to Dr Kilpatrick, then, that the bread and wine were holy things, holy in a positive and even potentially alarming sense. To become so, they had to be lifted out of the common run and placed in God's peculiar possession, so that for a man to partake of them was a privilege fenced about with sanctities. What, then, was held to hallow things like food or drink in such a way? Dr Kilpatrick gives the classical answer: it was offering in sacrifice to God that thus hallowed. And, he goes on to say, there is no difficulty about applying his answer to the Eucharist, for it had a sacrificial character from the first. The Lord declared the cup to be the new covenant in his blood. No blood could seal a covenant, but blood of sacrifice; it was with such blood that the old covenant had become sealed. Moreover the whole setting of the Last Supper, being paschal, was sacrificial. And, of course, in 1 Cor. 10. 16-21 St Paul explicitly compares the Christian Eucharist with sacrifices both pagan and Jewish.

But now at the point where Dr Kilpatrick's exposition touches the very spirit of St Paul's text, it loses contact with the letter. How can we say that St Paul's churches consecrated bread or wine by offering

---

[1] St Paul does mention disrespect for God's congregation, but it is in commenting on the detail of the misbehaviour, not in setting forth the alarming sin of sacrilege. "Have you not houses of your own to eat and drink in? Have you so little respect for the congregation of God that you let those who have not [houses of their own] feel their inferiority?"

it to God, when, to all evidence, they did not offer it at all? At a later time when the people's gifts were brought to the altar purely for sacramental or for charitable use, it was very natural they should be seen as oblations. But St Paul's Christians brought their dinner to the ecclesia, to eat it with their neighbours after due graces said. They did not offer anything; nor is there any suggestion of any such action, either in the Institution-Narrative or in St Paul's comments.

But though Dr Kilpatrick has not made the exposition fit the text, he has come so near to doing it that only a slight shift is needed for the pieces to fall into place. When he says that offering effected consecration, his statement has the ring of evident truth. Things became sacred by becoming God's peculiar possession, and they were made so by being given over to God. Once the gift had been brought into the Temple, let alone laid on the altar, it was considered irrevocable, and sacred to deity. The irrevocability, if not the physical sanctity, of the gift could be stretched much further back, as we can see from the Gospel discussions about *korban.* Property vowed to the ultimate service of the altar became from the moment of the vow *tabu* for any other use.

To offer, then, was to consecrate; and yet nothing could meaningfully be offered unless it was to be received. The appropriation of the gift to God was made absolute by his taking it. His altar devoured the sacrifice symbolically; such symbolic consumption expressing God's real acceptance of his people's offerings, long after they had outlived the barbarous belief that deity was nourished by the steam of burning flesh.

According to St Matthew, Christ had made two distinct protests against rabbinic exaggeration about the sanctity of offerings. They were wrong to stretch that sanctity so far that property vowed to God became exempt from the claims of human duty; and they were wrong to place such intrinsic holiness in the offering as to exalt it above the holiness of the altar. How could they treat an oath by the offering as binding—that is, as equivalent to an oath by the Divine Name—and an oath by the altar as not thus binding? For, said Christ, it is the altar that sanctifies the gift; the altar, we must suppose, being representative of God as recipient of the gift (Matt. 23. 18, 19).

It is a short step from such teaching to the language of 1 Cor. 10. 18, 20. "Look at the historical Israel. Are not those who eat the

3

sacrifices sharers with the altar? . . . What [your heathen neighbours] sacrifice, they sacrifice to demons and not to God; and I would not have you become sharers with demons. You cannot drink the cup of the Lord [Jesus] and the cup of demons, you cannot have part in the table of the Lord and in the table of demons."

The Jewish belief was that demons were the actual recipients of sacrifices vainly offered before statues of imaginary gods. So idolatry opened up a baleful commerce with demons, even though "an idol is nothing in the world, nor are idol-sacrifices anything", as St Paul says in this place. As recipients, the demons come into parallel with the altar at Jerusalem. The heathen taste the cup the demons taste, they partake the table demons partake, and so they are *sharers with* demons; as worshippers in the Temple are *sharers with* the altar, an altar representative of the Lord JHVH; and as Christian communicants are sharers with the Lord Christ.

A careless reading of St Paul's words may leave us with the impression that the altar is compared not with the Lord Jesus, but with his table. In fact it is not so; the table is indeed mentioned, but in another connexion. The whole sequence is as follows. The Apostle begins by mentioning a "sharing of the body and blood of Christ" as a privilege incompatible with idolatrous feasting. He proceeds to quote the standard, and, as it were, neutral example of the temple-sacrifices, to establish the general principle that those who eat things sacrificed have communion with their deity, though in Israel the claim must be qualified: they are "sharers with the Altar". He then makes the application to idolatry, and is forced to qualify again: idolaters are sharers, not with imaginary deities, but with all-too-real demons. Now at length he can, without the fear of misunderstanding, confront the demons with Christ. "You cannot drink the cup of the Lord and the cup of demons; you cannot partake of the Lord's table and the table of demons." The table is here simply the place of the bread, as the cup is the container of the wine. He might as well have said "platter" as "table", if they had eaten bread from platters; which I suppose they did not.

The facts of Israel's religion oblige St Paul to qualify the second limb of his parallel, and limit communion with the divine to "communion with the altar"; but it is unnecessary to suppose that the qualification is any embarrassment to the Apostle. Would he have preferred to place communion with Christ in direct parallel to communion with God? We can scarcely think so. The common form of New Testament theology is to describe the divine function or dignity of Christ as the reality figured in those quasi-representatives for God in which Jewish speech abounded—the Wisdom, the Word, the Glory, the Angel; and so why not, in a somewhat special context, the altar? By means of his altar, the Divine Majesty ate with his people "typically"; he ate with them bodily through his Son.

Well but, according to Dr Jeremias and other scholars, Christ did not eat with his disciples at all; he fasted through the Last Supper. My first observation on this head will be that St Paul had not read Dr Jeremias; even if the Professor, by the use of special learning, has correctly reconstructed what happened at the Supper, St Paul's knowledge was that of the current Church tradition, which he cites, and which leaves one to suppose that the Lord Jesus acted normally in the ceremonies of grace, by tasting what he proceeded to pass round. If St Paul had a more detailed picture of what had happened, it is still more probable that it was in rough agreement with the Synoptic Evangelists, than with a contradictory picture conjured out of a selection of their words by modern learning. All the Evangelists, taken as they stand, give us to understand that Christ ate the Supper, and most emphatically of all St Luke, who is made to vote the other way by a truly outrageous piece of exegesis. "How I have longed to eat this Passover with you before I suffered!" The expression "longed to . . .", we are told, is three times elsewhere used by St Luke, and always with the meaning "longed to, but could not"; and so the text before us must be read accordingly. One could scarcely find a more shocking example of the substitution of counting for thinking. "Longed to . . ." in Greek has exactly the sense it bears in English. Its employment always raises the question "And what was to stop him?" The question is to be answered out of the immediate context; we are not free to make up an answer to please ourselves. The Prodigal Son "longed to satisfy his hunger with the husks the swine ate".—And what was to stop him?—"A man cannot actually eat the Syrian equivalent of beech-mast". Lazarus "longed to eat the broken food from the rich man's table". And what was to stop him?—"Perhaps they would not let him have any; and they did not". Christ "longed to eat the Passover with his disciples *before he suffered*".—And what was to stop him?—"Having to suffer before Passover; but he did not". That is the answer, not "a vow he had taken against tasting a single morsel", as Dr Jeremias would have it. He did not have to suffer before he could eat Passover, and so there he was, eating it with them, according to the request he sent to the householder, "Where is the room for me to eat the Passover in with my disciples?"

Christ proceeds to explain the eagerness of the longing he has felt: "For I tell you, I will no more eat passover with you until it is fulfilled in the kingdom of God". This present Passover is their last together, that is its crucial significance; and the words about the cup, directly following, must be read in the same sense.

St Mark (from whom St Matthew does not relevantly diverge) is less clear and emphatic than St Luke. Certainly, however, nothing comes up in his story suggestive of abstinence, until the end of the Institution, where after the words about the cup we read the pro-testation : "No more will I drink the produce of the vine, to the day I drink it new with you in the Kingdom of God". The protestation may well have, as Dr Jeremias urges, the force of a vow—a vow which Christ proceeds to keep by refusing the drugged wine at his crucifixion; and of which Providence spares him even the involun-tary breach, by relieving him of his life just when a soldier is going to squeeze the vinegar into his dying mouth. But there is no warrant whatever for supposing that the vow (if such it was) forbade Christ's tasting "their last cup together" before he uttered it.

I have spent time enough in setting aside a theory which should never have been propounded. I pass on to what is perhaps the chief recommendation of the line we are pursuing : the light it throws on the declaration of Jesus that what he hands to his disciples in bread and wine is to be received as his body and blood. Consider the verses in 1 Corinthians 10 immediately preceding those we discussed above. "The cup of blessing which we bless, is it not our sharing in Christ's blood? The loaf we break, is it not our sharing in Christ's body? Because the loaf is one, we many are one body, for we all partake of the one loaf." It is the last sentence here which discloses the Apostle's drift. It was not proper that every man at supper should say his own grace; one grace was said, and all were drawn into it by eating a crumb of the one loaf over which it had been pronounced; and so again with the cup. A unity of body was created between the participants, through their all solemnly recruiting their bodies from the one loaf; but especially between the rest of them and the Father of the Feast, whose blessed loaf they partook.

It may be urged that the sharing was nevertheless reciprocal; that if Peter was made one body with Christ by the shared loaf, so was Christ with Peter. And while one remains on a purely natural level, it is so. But that is a level on which St Paul does not remain. The partaking in holy body and in holy blood is a one-way relationship; for the Son of God is the bearer of the divine life, and Peter is not.

Such appears to be St Paul's thought. The common Christian imagination may revolt. No, we may say, Christ gives us our share in his body and his blood by dying for us, not by eating with us. But suppose St Paul's imagination did not work like ours. We need not, however, exaggerate the difference. For him, as for us, Christ's body would not be the saving benefit it is to his people, if by self-oblation on the Cross it had not vanquished the enemy; nor would his blood be the price and seal of a new covenant, if it had never been spilt. Christ gave them his body at the Supper as that which was to stand in for them and his blood as that which should seal his covenant with them. He gave them the sacrament by eating with them; he made it their salvation by his death.

But we are going outside our subject. We digressed for the purpose of showing that St Paul's comparison of Eucharist and Sacrifice is such as to make the bread and wine Christ tasted at the Supper not only to be hallowed or consecrated in the fullest sense, but also to be for his disciples a sharing in his body and his blood. Let us return for a moment to the comparison itself. Evidently in drawing it St Paul is looking at sacrifice in general with the eyes of a Christian communicant; and his doing so has led him to select a pattern from the total complex of sacrificial ideas, to state which is virtually to redefine sacrifice as such. What is this implied definition? "Sacrifice is a solemn ceremony in which the deity deigns to receive earthly nourishment and to let his worshippers share in it". We will not brave the censure of anthropologists by offering this as an essential, still less a comprehensive definition of sacrifice; but we will hazard the claim that it uncovers deep and ancient roots of attitude and belief; for it springs from men's instinctive feelings about the bodily bond created by a common meal. Such elemental attitudes persist, even when overlaid by cultural sophistication; the ancient in a case like this turns out to be the human and familiar.

Having observed St Paul's sacrificial comparison, we may be moved to ask after the difference. Why is the Christian sacrament said to be a sharing in Christ's body and blood, whereas no such thing is said either of the pagan sacrifices, or of those in the Jewish Temple? The answer is plain. Neither the demon, nor the God of Israel is present in body and blood to eat with the worshippers. Communion in body and blood is communion with a divine life in-carnate. The thought is not developed by St Paul, but expands freely in the mind of St John. The Word made flesh, the Son of Man come down from heaven, is the bread that gives life to the world. Once the incarnation is understood, the sacrament is no stumblingblock.

St Paul does not develop the thought as St John develops it, but it is clear that he sets Jesus on the side of the divine—to communicate with him is like communicating with the altar of God. Jesus was nevertheless flesh and blood, sitting at table with his fellow-diners; and it was for this reason that he could take the initiative in an act of table-fellowship with them. Where the divine person—or the impersoned altar, say which you will—actually eats with the fellow-ship, the feast is consecrated *ipso facto*, and the question "What should they do to consecrate it?" simply does not arise. The concern with human forms of consecration belongs to the common pattern of sacrifice, where the divine participant is not visibly present nor unmistakeably active; his worshippers being anxious to know what conditions realizable by them will justify them in presuming his participation. If they present the offering in the hallowed place with the customary words, if they throw the acceptable portions into the altar fire. . . . Such concerns as these had no place at the Last Supper.

Jesus had been present in flesh and blood at Jerusalem in the upper room, he was not so present in the ecclesia at Corinth; and some-thing like the common sacrificial situation was bound, therefore, to reconstitute itself. What had they to do, to assure his partici-pation? He had told them—they were to do what he had done in blessing, distributing, partaking; and if they did so, they took it that every eucharist they held was the Supper of the Lord, instinct with the added virtue of Christ's resurrection.

Perhaps they would have said that all they did according to his command was equivalent to what he had done with his disciples. If we press a formula of this sort, we obtain the conclusion that the celebrant's tasting of the bread and wine is equivalent to Christ's tasting of them, and as such constitutes the essential and uniquely consecrating moment. The conclusion may be logical; it can never have been spiritually acceptable. The celebrant must know himself to receive the Lord's body and blood along with his fellow-Christians; he cannot, at that moment, see himself as acting in the person of the Divine. It is in saying the blessing that he can so act. He who prays on behalf of the Holy Church becomes the voice and instrument of her divine and human Head.

Here is a line of sacramental reflection bound to prevail, because it finds an ally in the attitude of the worshipper; and the working out of it gave the Church in due course her liturgy, with the theology interpretative of it. We have no good reason to suppose that the development was yet under way when St Paul wrote to Corinth. Living in the aftermath of Resurrection and in the eve of Advent, they were content to do among themselves what Christ had done with his disciples. We for our part cannot reverse the current of history, or return to Pauline usages. But it may comfort us to observe that the highest elaboration of sacramental theology need not obscure the Pauline faith. It was pure Paulinism which St Thomas wrote into his famous stanza :

> By birth their fellowman was he,
> Their meat in sharing their repast;
> He died their ransom-price to be,
> He reigns, their recompense at last.

3

THE EUCHARIST IN THE THOUGHT
OF THE EARLY CHURCH

G. W. H. LAMPE

"Had St Paul heard the phrase 'the Blessed Sacrament'," it has been remarked, "he would have thought it meant Baptism". There is some truth in the joke; for in the early Church's missionary situation, apologetic and evangelistic writing (which includes a very high proportion of early Christian literature) naturally focused its attention on the sacrament of conversion and "illumination", the mystery of rebirth to eternal life, the initiation of which the subsequent course of the convert's entire life in the Church was a fulfilment and working out.

This is one reason why references to the Eucharist in the pre-Nicene period, though frequent, are relatively scattered, unsystematic, and allusive. There is nothing corresponding to Tertullian's treatise on Baptism, and it is not until the fourth century that we find detailed information about the teaching given to catechumens about the Eucharist; and the evidence for the structure and content of the early liturgies themselves is comparatively scanty. The strong third-century tendency to present the Christian sacraments as true counterparts of the false pagan mysteries, and consequently to conceal the details of them from the uninitiated, is a contributory factor, but not of great significance: it applied in some degree to Baptism also. The chief reason for the paucity of theological expositions of the Eucharist in the early period, and the reason why the Christian writers' occasional allusions to it are difficult to analyse systematically, is that the Eucharist stands at the heart of the early Church's faith and life; it embodies, and proclaims in a single rite, the entire richness of the gospel; and for this very reason it does not lend itself to precise definition or to clear-cut theories about presence, sacrifice, consecration, and the relation of the sacramental act and of the visible elements to the reality which they signify. Early Christian belief about the Eucharist is complex and, just because it is of both profound and far-ranging, it can only be misunderstood if the categories of later theology are applied to it and the early Fathers are made to answer questions which they were not concerned to ask.

In the background there stand Jewish meals of fellowship and blessings said at table, and, in particular, the Passover commemoration of redemption. For Christians the eucharistic meal is still the focus of their fellowship, the ground and expression of the Church's unity in Christ and of the love which binds it together, a rite still closely associated in idea with the ἀγάπη even though, after the earliest period, not actually attached to it. It is the community's corporate act of thanksgiving, and for Christians, who live by faith in the risen Lord, thanksgiving is centred upon commemoration of the saving events of Christ's death and resurrection by which men have been reconciled to God, and God's creation has been rescued from the dominion of evil and assured of the hope of restoration. Thanksgiving implies offering, for thanksgiving and sacrifice are correlated; and the Eucharist is the Church's offering of praise, blessing, self-dedication, and the expression of all this in practical service to the needy; for the "offering of the gifts" was the source and the symbol of the Church's provision for its poor and distressed members, the charitable relief which caused Polycarp to speak of the widows as "God's altar"[1] and which, as the Emperor Julian realized when it was too late, was a most important factor in the Church's victory over the pagan cults.[2]

Thanksgiving, however, was not a mere commemoration of God's past acts; it was centred upon present communion with the crucified and risen Lord. Thanksgiving to God was said over the loaf and cup (thereby hallowing or blessing—i.e., blessing God for—the bread and wine) of which the Lord had said, "This is my body", "This is my blood". In the Eucharist the communicant received the bread of heaven, the Lord himself, as the source and

[1] *ep*. 4. 9.
[2] Julian, *Gal*. 305B-D, *ep*. 49. On the interconnection between *diakonia* and eucharistic *leitourgia* I would refer to my essay, "Diakonia in the Early Church", McCord and Parker, *Service in Christ* (Epworth Press, 1966).

giver of eternal life. Here was a continual renewing of the baptismal incorporation into Christ, the individual believer feeding on the Lord of life and the Church being built up as his body; here, too, was the ground of the hope of resurrection of the whole man and of the consummation of union with Christ at the parousia when the Church would be gathered into God's Kingdom. In the Eucharist Christ's death and resurrection were made present to the faithful as contemporary realities in which they participated sacramentally and in which they shared, in a more tangible way, in the daily dying and rising with Christ which, according to much early Christian thought, found its proper fulfilment in martyrdom.

Since so much of what early writers say about the Eucharist is contained in occasional allusions, these often emphasize only one or two aspects of this complex faith, and circumstances lead certain theologians to lay special stress on particular elements in it: as, for example, Ignatius and Augustine on the Church's eucharistic unity (against schism), or Cyprian, in his concern with the "lapsed", on the dangers of the profanation of the sacrament by unworthy receivers. It would be wrong to assume that such writers held a one-sided view of the Eucharist. Since, too, the Eucharist is a sacrament of the whole gospel, it is sometimes difficult to determine whether a particular passage is eucharistic in the narrow sense or whether the author's thought has passed over into the wider sphere of the entire relationship of Christ with the believer. This is especially true in the case of Clement, and of Origen whose Platonism leads him constantly to penetrate beyond the visible sacrament to the spiritual apprehension of the Logos, the living bread, through the assimilation of his teaching and progressive sanctification.

No early writer leaves us in any doubt that the central reality which Christians encounter in the Eucharist is the living and life-giving presence and grace of the Lord in and with his people. The interest of the early Church, however, was in the reality of communion with Christ, participation in the bread of eternal life; it was not in attempting to define the way in which the elements are ontologically related to the life-giving body and blood. It is true that "symbolical" language about the elements is characteristic of many theologians, such as Tertullian and Augustine, and that a "conversionist" way of speaking becomes especially prominent in Greek theology during the fourth century and, through Ambrose, in the later West; but, at least until the middle of the fourth century and in the case of some theologians considerably later, the framework of thought is different from that in which the eucharistic teaching of John of Damascus, Radbert, Rabanus Maurus, Ratramn, Berengar, and Lanfranc moved. The questions that are being asked are not the same. It has often been pointed out that "symbolical" or "figurative" language is not incompatible with an underlying "realism"; to some extent it is also true that startlingly "realistic" language can accompany a basic acknowledgement of "symbolism".

This applies also to the concept of sacrifice. Many Reformation battles have been fought around Cyprian's statement that "the Lord's passion is the sacrifice we offer";[3] but Cyprian was not answering the questions of the sixteenth and later centuries. He was emphasizing the need to do nothing in the rite but what the Lord did: i.e., not to celebrate with water only, without wine. At every celebration, he says, we make mention of his passion : that is to say, the passion is the central subject of our sacrifice of thanksgiving, not simply as a past event but as a present reality (in which the believer may be called to share literally through martyrdom) and as the ground of our hope. This thanksgiving is offered over the cup; the cup is thereby blessed; and it is no long step which Cyprian takes when he goes on to speak of "offering the cup in commemoration of the Lord and his passion", or, as a parallel expression, "the Lord's passion is the sacrifice we offer". It is misleading to transfer Cyprian's language from the context of thanksgiving or thank-offering (εὐχαριστία) which dominated his own thinking, and use it to answer later questions about the precise sense in which the *elements* are offered in sacrifice, the mode in which they are made Christ's body and blood by consecration, and the relation of this sacrifice to the Cross. If the Early Fathers are treated as an ammunition dump for later eucharistic controversies (and the tendency to do so lingers on in this field of theology), the conclusion must be either that "all must have prizes" or that these writers were extraordinarily vague and even self-contradictory. In fact, what might appear to be vagueness is an indication of a richness of understanding.

This complexity makes it impossible to give a brief account of early eucharistic doctrine as a whole. It would require a full

[3] *ep.* 63. 17.

treatment of each author in all aspects of his teaching about the sacrament. It is therefore necessary to do what ought not to be done: to isolate the two aspects of the Eucharist which the Fathers held together and related to a wider context, that is to say, eucharistic presence and eucharistic sacrifice, and to take a bird's-eye glance at the teaching of certain Christian writers about each in turn.

I take the sacrificial aspect first because, while this is not explicitly present in the New Testament, it is a constant and universal theme in the patristic writings and it is understood in a wide range of meaning. As a background we should bear in mind Philo's spiritual interpretation of Old Testament sacrifices.[4] The kinds of victims prescribed by the Law signify moral qualities, and their perfection symbolizes the right disposition of those who come to pray or offer thanksgiving (εὐχαριστία). The morning and evening oblations are offered ἐν εὐχαριστία for the benefits received from God by night and day. Animal sacrifices are a εὐχαριστία for men's bodily selves, incense for their souls. Prayers and thanksgivings are offered, through the medium of sacrifices, in honour of God and for the benefit of the worshippers through their participation in good things and deliverance from what is evil. The burnt-offering denotes the total dedication of the soul to God; the division of the victim indicates that εὐχαριστία offered in thankfulness for the creation must include reference to all its constituent parts, sun, moon, stars, earth, animals, plants, and so on; that when it is offered for mankind it must refer in detail to men, women, Greeks, barbarians; and that εὐχαριστία for the individual must be made in respect of every element in his make-up: body, soul, reason, senses, etc. The conviction of Hellenistic Judaism that all sacrifice must ultimately be spiritual, and that it is primarily the grateful response of man to the Creator, is shared by the Church. Acceptable sacrifice is self-dedication, the Pauline "rational worship", praise, thanksgiving, prayer.

For Christians the offering of such sacrifices has been made possible by Christ's saving work. Commemoration of his passion and resurrection, participation by faith in his sufferings, and, through the assurance of hope, in his risen life are the ground and focus of the Church's εὐχαριστία. The sacramental rite thus stands

---

[4] *de victimis* 1-6.

at the heart of all Christian thanksgiving. But the spiritual sacrifice of grateful response is not confined to the liturgical action; the term εὐχαριστία and its cognate verb are very often applied to prayer and praise of all kinds, and to the martyr's self-offering,[5] as well as to the sacrament, and the word "sacrifice" (θυσία) is used, for many centuries, of prayer, virtuous conduct, and martyrdom, almost as often as of the Eucharist. Clement of Rome calls Christ "the high priest of our offerings"[6] immediately after quoting Psalm 50. 23: "the sacrifice of praise shall glorify me". He is alluding to Christian devotion in general, but probably having in mind the Eucharist as well as other forms of spiritual offering, such as were typified by the Old Testament sacrifices.[7] When he goes on to speak of those "who have offered the gifts" being improperly "thrust out of their ἐπισκοπή",[8] he is certainly alluding to the liturgical function of the eucharistic celebrant. For although the whole rite is called *eucharistia* (since, as Chrysostom says,[9] it is a memorial of God's many benefits and shows forth the culmination of his providence towards men), εὐχαριστία denotes equally the bread and wine of the Supper which are the thankoffering *par excellence*. It was the task of the celebrant to receive the offerings of bread and wine, with the gifts that furnished resources for the relief of the needy, and to offer the congregation's prayer of thanksgiving over the bread and the cup, by which these elements were hallowed and made the sacraments of Christ's body and blood. To "offer [the gifts]" is a regular technical term for "celebrate the Eucharist".

As early as the Didache (probably not later than the first years of the second century) the Eucharist is the sacrifice[10] which, by replacing the Jewish sacrifices and by being offered throughout the world, fulfils Malachi's prophecy of the pure oblation:[11] a text which plays an important part in Justin's arguments against Trypho[12] and constantly recurs in later writers. The themes of the thanksgiving in the Didache concerning the cup and bread, and those of the thanksgiving after the meal (possibly the ἀγάπη) are

[5] Clem. *str.* 4. 21. 130.
[6] 1 Clem. 36. 1.
[7] Ibid. 40, 41.
[8] Ibid. 44. 4 (curiously mistranslated by Lightfoot, "the gifts of the bishop's office").
[9] *hom.* 25. 3 *in Mt.*
[10] Didache 14. 1.
[11] Ibid. 1. 11.
[12] dial. 41, 17.

similar: the vine of David revealed in Christ is the subject of the
blessing over the cup; over the bread, the life and knowledge made
known through Jesus, with prayer that the Church may be gathered
together into God's Kingdom as the grains of wheat have been
assembled in one loaf; thanksgiving after the meal is offered for the
indwelling of God's name in our hearts, for knowledge, faith, and
immortality revealed in Jesus, for material food and drink, and for
the gift of spiritual food and drink and eternal life through God's
Son, and for the mightiness of God; prayer is again made for the
eschatological ingathering of the Church into the Kingdom, concluding with an affirmation of the Church's expectation of the
parousia (*maranatha*).[13] There is no explicit reference here to
Christ's saving work except in terms of revelation, and no allusion
to the Institution and the passion. The Didache is also distinctive
in its very close association of thanksgiving with eschatological
assurance; in the fourth century the idea of the loaf as a symbol
of the gathering together of the Church recurs in Sarapion,[14] no
longer as the future ingathering of Church into Kingdom but rather
as the building-up of the community in the present age. In its connection of the creation of material things with re-creation for
eternal life, however, this thanksgiving is typical of the early
Eucharist (cf. Justin. *dial.* 118). In this corporate act of thanksgiving
there is grounded the unity and peace of the Church: a primary
theme in Ignatius.[15] Not only the entire action but the actual bread
and cup are seen by Justin as the sacrifices offered by the Gentiles
in Malachi's prophecy;[16] for bread, and wine mixed with water,
become the thankoffering (εὐχαριστία) when the thanksgiving has
been said over them and they have thus been "eucharistized".[17] This
thanksgiving is offered for creation and redemption, with the
central emphasis on the commemoration of Christ's passion. The
bread of the Eucharist is that with which Christ taught us to make
a memorial of his blood in giving thanks.[18] The Eucharist is thus a

---

[13] Didache 9, 10.

[14] *euchol.* 13.

[15] E.g., *Eph.* 13. 1.

[16] *dial.* 41, 17.

[17] *1 apol.* 65, 66.

[18] *dial.* 41. 1; 70. 4. Justin's curious expression in these passages, [(ἄρτος)]
ὃν παρέδωκεν ἡμῖν ... Χριστὸς ποιεῖν εἰς ἀνάμνησιν τοῦ πάθους, κτλ., is sometimes translated, "the bread (and the cup) which Christ taught us to sacrifice in memory
of . . ." This may be possible, but it is doubtful if ποιεῖν, without an object

sacrifice in the sense that it fulfils Malachi's prophecy of a new worship superseding the Levitical rites, and as the sacrifice of thanksgiving in which the blessings of creation, and Christ's saving work, in its present redemptive power, are commemorated.

Thanksgiving for creation, the "harvest-festival" aspect of the Eucharist, appeals most strongly to Irenaeus. It supplies him with a powerful weapon against Gnostic and Marcionite dualism. The offering of bread and wine does not mean that the Lord stands in need of anything; it is made in thanksgiving for creation and as a sanctification of created things. We offer to God what is his own, and thereby proclaim the union of flesh with spirit.[19]

Tertullian sets the eucharistic sacrifice in its wider context: the rendering of glory to God, blessing, praise, and hymns are all included in Malachi's "pure oblation";[20] so are all the spiritual sacrifices of Christians.[21] Within this framework he applies the term *offerre* more specifically to the Eucharist,[22] and he mentions among the unwritten traditions of his time the making of "oblations" for the departed,[23] no doubt alluding to the commemoration of the dead at the eucharistic thanksgiving offered on their anni-

which in itself connotes a sacrifice, ought to be rendered "to sacrifice". Justin has probably conflated the narrative of the Last Supper and the words of Institution, and it is likely that ἄρτον ποιεῖν εἰς ἀνάμνησιν τοῦ πάθους means the same as ἄρτῳ ἀνάμνησιν ποιεῖν τοῦ πάθους "make a memorial of the passion with bread". ἀνάμνησις is not in itself a sacrificial or specifically eucharistic term and ἀνάμνησιν ποιεῖν means "commemorate" or "make a memorial of". Dix is misleading when, in his translation of the *Apostolic Tradition*, he renders *quando hoc facitis, meam commemorationem facitis* (ποιεῖτε (εἰς) τὴν ἐμὴν ἀνάμνησιν) by "when ye do this, ye do my "anamnesis", and *memores igitur mortis* (μεμνημένοι τοίνυν τοῦ θανάτου) by "doing therefore the 'anamnesis' of his death", instead of by "you make my memorial (or commemoration)", and "commemorating therefore his death". Baptism is equally an ἀνάμνησις of the passion (Methodius. *symp.* 3. 8; 8. 6), as is the Friday fast (Eusebius, *pasch.* 12); and the distribution of alms out of a dead person's estate is made εἰς ἀνάμνησιν αὐτοῦ "for a memorial or commemoration of him" (*Apostolic Constitutions* 8. 42. 5. This is not to deny that "commemoration" in a eucharistic context means a recollection of a past event so that its consequences take effect in the present (Dix, *The Apostolic Tradition of Hippolytus*, p. 73), nor that this recollection is before both God and men. Hence in the context of the Eucharist the idea has sacrificial overtones, since the sacrifice offered to God is the thankful recollection of the saving work of Christ in its present and efficacious reality.

19 *haer.* 4. 18. 4.
20 *adv. Marc.* 3. 22.
21 *adv. Jud.* 5.
22 *cult. fem.* 2. 11, etc.
23 *cor. mil.* 3.

versaries. Cyprian speaks of this in slightly more detail: he tells us that sacrifices are offered for certain martyrs whom he names, "as often as we celebrate the passions of the martyrs and their days [of martyrdom] with an anniversary commemoration".[24] Cyprian does not seem to imply that these Eucharists have an intercessory character, for he is expatiating on the "palms and crowns" which the martyrs have already won. The sacrifice is more probably thought of as consisting in the linking of the martyrs' passions with the passion of Christ commemorated in the thanksgiving at every Eucharist.

This commemoration involves making mention of the passion in every Eucharist,[25] and also the sacramental representation or imitation of Christ's action at the Last Supper. Hence Cyprian's objection to the use of water without wine; for it was a mixed cup which the Lord offered and it was wine which he said was his blood, and if this element is lacking the blood of Christ is not offered.[26] The priest performs the part of Christ if he imitates what Christ did, and offers a true sacrifice to God in the Church if he offers in accordance with Christ's offering.[27] "Doing what the Lord did" means offering the mixed cup in commemoration of the passion.[28] It must be mixed, because, as wine signifies the blood of Christ, so water is a sign of the Church in its union with him. The mixed cup, in which neither wine nor water exists without the other, is parallel to the loaf, compounded of flour and water, which signifies the unity of the Church in Christ, the heavenly bread.[29] Here is an idea which goes back through the Didache (where, however, it is eschatological) to St Paul, and was greatly developed by Augustine. Christ's sacrifice can be celebrated only in the Church; schismatics profane the truth of the "dominical victim" by offering false sacrifices (i.e., celebrating a Eucharist which is not authentic);[30] for the eucharistic commemoration shows forth the union of the Church with Christ, the one bread of life. All this is again placed by Cyprian in a wider context. Confessors who cannot celebrate the

[24] ep. 39. 3.
[25] ep. 63. 17.
[26] Ibid., 9.
[27] Ibid., 14.
[28] Ibid., 17.
[29] Ibid., 13.
[30] eccl. un. 17.

divine sacrifices offer an equally precious sacrifice of themselves; this is the best form of thanksgiving for God's benefits.[31]

The thanksgiving is centred upon the work of Christ; and the anaphora of the *Apostolic Tradition* of Hippolytus opens directly with praise for the sending of Christ in the Incarnation, without any mention of creation (though the latter may have been originally present). Nevertheless, the "harvest-festival" theme continues to be prominent. "We give thanks to the Creator of the universe," says Origen, "and eat the loaves that are presented with thanksgiving and prayer over the gifts, so that by the prayer they become a certain holy body which sanctifies those who partake of it with a pure intention".[32] At the same time a development is taking place in the idea of sacrifice: the eucharistic commemoration of Christ's death, with which is linked the worshippers' self-dedication, has a propitiatory effect towards God, and thus supersedes the Levitical offerings.[33] In the offering of the bread and the cup there is, according to Sarapion's anaphora,[34] a "likeness" of Christ's death, and prayer is made that God may be propitiated through this sacrifice (θυσία). The introduction of a propitiatory motive into the sacrifice, and its interpretation in terms of a re-presentation, rather than a commemoration only, of the passion, was bound to have a profound effect on the concept of sacrifice, even though the patristic writers avoided precise definition and combined, rather than distinguished, differing interpretations. It is naturally led to questions about the relation of the eucharistic action to the sacrifice of Calvary.

Cyril of Jerusalem sets out this propitiatory interpretation more fully, and relates it to the intercessions for the dead, these being especially effective for their souls "when the holy and most awful sacrifice is set forth".[35] This change of emphasis is connected with the growing tendency in the fourth century to use "conversionist" language in speaking of the consecration of the elements. It does not mean, however, a reproduction of the sacrifice of the cross. The former, according to Gregory Nazianzen, is an "antitype" (i.e., an outward form corresponding to a heavenly reality).[36] Chrysostom speaks

31 *ep.* 76. 3.
32 *Cels.* 8. 33.
33 Origen. *hom.* 13. 3, 4 *in Lev.;* ibid., 9. 10.
34 13.
35 *catech.* 23. 8, 9.
36 *or.* 2. 95.

with startling realism about the eucharistic sacrifice: "You are approaching an awful and holy sacrifice; Christ is set before you slain",[37] but in a less rhetorical mood he interprets sacrifice in terms of commemoration : "We do not offer another sacrifice but the same [as Christ's]; or rather, we make a memorial (ἀνάμνησις) of the sacrifice".[38] His more precise teaching is echoed by Theodore of Mopsuestia,[39] and by Theodoret: "We commemorate that one saving sacrifice".[40] Theodoret also develops the idea of Christ offering to the Father in the Eucharist in and through his body, the Church.[41] In the West a "realistic" and propitiatory understanding of the sacrifice is markedly present in Ambrose. Christ is present at our sacrifice; Christ, our passover, is imolated.[42] Christ is offered on earth when his body is offered; he offers in us when his word consecrates the sacrifice that is offered, while at the same time he intercedes for us in heaven.[43]

On the other hand, Augustine dwells more particularly on the thought of the Eucharist as a mystery of the Church in union with its Head. The true bread is in heaven; his body, the Church, is here, a loaf made of many grains, ground by exorcisms and fasting, compacted by baptism and baked by the fire of the Spirit. God wills us to be his sacrifice, and in the eucharistic offering his sacrifice is consecrated.[44] The oblation is our vow to abide in Christ, in the unity of his body, of which the Eucharist is a sacrament because we who are many are one bread, one body.[45] Hence to communicate is synonymous with "to offer".[46] It is the privilege of the body to give thanks to God; hence in the sacrifice we are told, "Let us give thanks to our Lord God".[47] The Church's self-offering is part and parcel of the thankoffering which commemorates Christ's oblation. Christ is immolated daily; but this is done by our thankful remembrance

---

37 *prod. Jud.* 2. 6; cf. *sac.* 3. 4; 6. 4.
38 *hom.* 17. 3 *in Heb.*
39 *catech.* 15. 15.
40 *Heb.* 8. 5.
41 *Ps.* 109. 4.
42 *exp. in Lc.* 1. 28.
43 *enarr. in Ps.* 38. 25.
44 *serm.* 227.
45 *ep.* 149. 16.
46 Ibid., 54. 2.
47 Ibid., 187. 20, 21.

of his benefits.[48] Augustine is careful to say that to speak of this daily immolation is legitimate because a sacrament, by virtue of its resemblance to what it signifies, may receive the name which properly belongs to the reality signified.[49] Augustine generally avoids the tendency to give a propitiatory significance to the eucharistic sacrifice, the source of so much later confusion. Only in connexion with the offering of the sacrifice of Christ, and the sacrifice of alms, on behalf of the dead, does he hesitate about this: for the very good they are thanksgivings, but for the not very bad they are propitiations.[50] Whereas, too, in the East "the sacrifice" was increasingly coming to mean "the consecrated elements" (occasionally, too, the elements before consecration[51]), and, later, even "communion" came to be used in this sense,[52] Augustine often applies the term to the entire rite.[53]

Augustine's very rich doctrine of sacrifice is echoed by later Western writers. According to Ratramn, Christ can be said to be immolated when the sacrament of his passion is celebrated, though in himself he was immolated once. He does not suffer daily what he performed once; but he left us an example (1 Peter 2. 21) which is daily presented to believers in the eucharistic mystery. Christ offered himself once, but this same oblation is daily celebrated in a mystery, through the commemoration of his passion. Because the sacrament resembles and represents his death and passion, Christ can rightly be said to be immolated or to suffer in the mysteries.[54] By now, however, the precise relationship of the Eucharist to the cross has become a controversial question. Radbertus seems to hold that Christ indeed died once for the world's salvation, but, in the daily commemoration which we effect by sacrificing his body and blood on the altar, Christ is daily sacrificed for us mystically as a propitiation for our continuing sins and for the infirmity of sin which persists in the flesh;[55] and he reinforces his teaching with popular legends, largely culled from Gregory, telling of the miraculous efficacy of the eucharistic sacrifice as a propitiation for the living

---

48 *enarr. in Ps.* 75. 15.
49 *ep.* 98. 9.
50 *oct. Dulcit. quaest.* 2. 4.
51 E.g., in the *Liturgy of the Apostolic Constitutions* 8. 10. 2.
52 E.g., John Moschus, *prat.* 79.
53 E.g., *spir. et. litt.* 18.
54 *de corp. et. sang. Dom.* 38-40.
55 *de corp. et. sang. Dom.* 9. 1.

and the dead.[56] Lanfranc also insists, against Berengar's Augustinian-ism, that, although Christ was immolated once in himself, his flesh is daily immolated, divided, and eaten.[57] All this controversy is remote from the faith of the early centuries.

Early Christian thought about the eucharistic Presence and consecration naturally develops along the same lines. From the first there was no doubt that in the bread and the cup over which thanksgiving has been offered there is received the life-giving pre-sence of the bread which came down from heaven to give life to the world and which had been typified by the manna, and the blood of his reconciling sacrifice which had been prefigured by the water from the rock which was Christ. The Eucharist is a sacrament (often described by such terms as τύπος, ἀντίτυπον, *figura*) which *is* dynamically, i.e., in grace and power rather than in substance, that which it signifies. It is only when such questions as "how can this be Christ's body, seeing that it appears to be bread?" begin to be asked and answered, as by Cyril of Jerusalem, that the way is opened to the subtle controversies of the ninth and eleventh centuries.

The mode by which the elements are thus identified with what they signify could be thought of in terms of the power of the Word, with particular reference to Christ's words of Institution and the imitation of his actions and words in the Church, of the action of the Spirit supervening upon the elements, or of the infusion of divine power into them, parallel to the sanctification of baptismal water. However it might be explained, the elements become "holy" and channels of divine energy. Within the Church's general belief there are differences of emphasis. They range from Origen's very clear distinction between the elements as such and the true spiritual food, the Logos (made available to the faithful through the word of prayer said over the bread and cup), to the literalistic piety which led Marcus the Valentinian to perform conjuring tricks to make the contents of the cup look like blood,[58] and even the much more respectable theologian, Cyprian, to credit horror stories about the behaviour of the sacred elements when they were profaned by the hands or lips of unreconciled apostates.[59]

---

[56] Ibid., 9. 8ff.
[57] *de. sacr. corp. et. sang. Christi.* 15.
[58] Iren. *haer.* 1. 13. 2.
[59] *laps.* 25, 26.

The question which largely remains unspoken is, "what is meant by the 'body and blood of Christ' in the context of the Eucharist?" The implicit answer of Clement and Origen is, "The Logos, apprehended by faith", this being understood primarily as the absorption of his teaching. This view enables communion, like sacrifice, to be seen in the wider framework of a variety of modes of spiritual feeding upon the Word. Often, however, the implied answer is given in terms of a more physical concept, so that Christ's body and blood can be thought of as nourishment for the physical life of man, i.e., as assuring the body of future resurrection, or, in later Greek terminology, as "divinizing" it, while, as Tertullian says, "the soul is fed by God".[60] With the clearer assertion of fourth century writers that the eucharistic body is actually identical with the body born of Mary and crucified, belief in the incorporation of the faithful into Christ's body through the Eucharist, and their divinization through participation in the flesh of the Logos, made eucharistic belief a central underlying factor in the Christological controversies. When this assertion, in turn, gave rise to matter-of-fact questions about how the body in heaven can be eaten on earth, the speculations of Radbert and Ratramn began to anticipate the Reformation disputes about "ubiquity" and the *extra Calvinisticum*. But although it would have been better if the unspoken question had been brought into the open, it is clear that the general belief of the early Church, emphasized especially by Irenaeus, is that man, in body and soul, is fed by Christ, the bread of eternal life, and, as Ignatius and Augustine so strongly maintain, the Church is constituted as Christ's body, and given unity, in his life which finds its expression in mutual love.

Ignatius is typical of a strong "realism" which yet moves in a different sphere from the medieval doctrines. The Eucharist is the flesh of Christ which suffered and was raised; at the same time this flesh is the principle of the Church's unity, which is broken by schism.[61] The bread of God, as opposed to the food of corruption (identified with the pleasures of this life) is the flesh of Christ who is of the seed of David; his blood is incorruptible love.[62] The one bread that is broken is the "medicine of immortality, the remedy

[60] *res. carn.* 8.
[61] *Smyrn.* 6. 2; *Philad.* 4.
[62] *Rom.* 7. 3.

that we should not die but live for ever in Christ".[63] This sounds materialistic and even magical; but the way in which Ignatius balances the historical realism of "the flesh of Christ of the seed of David" with the "spiritualism" of "the blood of Christ which is love" suggests that to accuse him of crude materialism would be unfair.[64] He probably means simply that communion with Christ in the Eucharist is the assurance of resurrection : the belief of the early Church as a whole.

Justin, having described the liturgical offering and the celebrant's eucharistic prayer, speaks of the distribution of bread and of wine and water, over which thanksgiving has been made ("eucharistized"). These are not received as ordinary food and drink, but just as Christ became incarnate in flesh and blood through the word of God, so the "eucharistized" food, which, *qua* material, nourishes our flesh and blood by physical conversion, is believed to be the flesh and blood of Jesus who was incarnate.[65] This parallel between the bodily and spiritual effects of the sacraments often recurs in later writers. The "word of prayer from him" by which the elements are made to become Eucharist is the thanksgiving, and in particular the words of Institution therein repeated (as in all liturgies save "Addai and Mari"). Irenaeus speaks in a similar way. He is especially insistent that it is a material object, earthly bread, which, having received the invocation (ἐπίκλησις) of God, thenceforth bears a dual character, earthly and heavenly; and that man's physical nature obtains eternal life through partaking of it.[66] The bearing of this on his anti-Marcionite and anti-Gnostic polemic is obvious.

Tertullian shares the same belief that in Communion the Lord's body is received, and may, indeed, be reserved at home for private Communion.[67] The manner of its reception is sacramental. In calling bread his body, says Tertullian, Christ makes us understand that he

---

[63] *Eph.* 20.

[64] Ignatius' metaphor of "medicine" (φάρμακον), repeated in Sarapion's "medicine of life" (*euchol.* 15) and Gregory Nazianzen's description of the Eucharist as a medicine which anoints the whole body (*or.* 8. 18) is not uncommon. The "word which induces repentance" is the medicine of immortality (Clem. *prot.* 10. 106); Theodoret calls Baptism the medicine of salvation (*Is.* 10. 23); and Clement says that water, as opposed to strong drink, is the medicine of temperance (*paed.* 2. 2. 20).

[65] *1 apol.* 65, 66.

[66] *haer.* 4. 18. 4; cf. 4. 33. 2; 5. 2. 2, 3.

[67] *pudic.* 9; *orat.* 19.

has given bread as a figure (*figura*) of his body. His institution of a sacrament of his body corresponds to the prophetic *pre*-figuring of his body by means of bread in the Old Testament (i.e., in Jer. 11. 19 (LXX) as a type of the crucifixion).[68] "This is my body" means "this is a figure (i.e., an effective symbol) of my body"; and the fact that Christ's body can have a *figura* implies, against Docetists, that his body was real. Christ's choice of the particular symbols of bread and wine is related to the typology of Jeremiah 11. 19; Isaiah 63. 1, and Genesis 49. 11.[69] Like Augustine, Tertullian has no doubt that the elements are dynamically and sacramentally Christ's body and blood; he is equally clear that they are not to be identified literally with that reality. Neither in the sacrament, however, nor in the Old Testament types, is the symbol merely a visual aid. Christ "represents" (*repraesentat*) his body by bread;[70] and for Tertullian *repraesentatio* means almost the same as "presence",[71] while *repraesentare* can mean "to present" on a stage.[72] Thus in the bread the dynamic actuality of Christ's body is presented.

Cyprian's teaching about eucharistic presence has already been mentioned in connexion with his ideas about sacrifice. The parallel, however, which he sees between the wine in the mixed cup as the sacrament of Christ's blood and the water as the sacrament of the Church must be borne in mind in considering his apparently literalistic assertion in the same passage that to drink the wine is to drink Christ's blood.[73] Water, in the Eucharist, is differently interpreted in Hippolytus' *Apostolic Tradition*.[74] According to the Latin version, the bread is distributed with the words, "The heavenly bread in Christ Jesus". It is the *similitudo* or "antitype" of Christ's flesh. Three cups (this is the post-baptismal Eucharist of the initiates) are then administered: of wine, the antitype of Christ's blood; of milk with honey, signifying the promise to the patriarchs; and of water. Each is administered thrice, in the Father, in Christ, and in the Spirit and (or in) the Church, recalling the

---

68 *adv. Marc.* 3. 19.
69 Ibid., 4. 40.
70 Ibid., 1. 14.
71 Tertullian contrasts *imagines in visione* with *veritates in repraesentatione* (*cor. mil.* 15).
72 *spect.* 17.
73 *ep.* 63. 13, 15.
74 23. 1-10.

baptismal interrogations; and the water appears to signify an inward baptism of the soul, corresponding to the external baptism of the body.

The common belief of the early Church is shared by Clement and Origen. Clement attacks those who "eucharistize" mere water.[75] He speaks of the blood of Christ in a way which makes it almost synonymous with "Spirit", and says that to drink of it is to partake of incorruptibility and to receive the Eucharist sanctifies body and soul.[76] He and Origen, however, always see sacramental Communion as an expression of a deeper reality: the total apprehension of the Logos by intellectual understanding and contemplation. For Origen it is not in itself the most advanced form of communion. The bread and the cup are for simpler people; the more instructed can receive the Word of truth more directly.[77] The "flesh and blood" of John 6 means primarily Christ's teaching, and later Origenists follow this exegesis: for instance, Eusebius,[78] and Evagrius who interprets "flesh and blood" as meaning Christ's whole incarnate life which, as a present reality, is mediated to believers through his teaching.[79]

Origen does indeed speak of the gifts becoming through prayer "a certain holy body",[80] but he leaves no doubt of the sharp distinction between the symbol and the reality. It is not what enters the mouth that sanctifies a man, even though simpler folk may think that what is called the Lord's bread sanctifies. What is consecrated by God's word and prayer does not of itself sanctify the recipient; otherwise the unworthy recipient would be sanctified by it. There is benefit to the man who receives it with a pure mind and conscience; but we neither suffer loss through not eating, nor are we the better for eating, as such. God's benefits come through righteous conduct; the consecrated food, *qua* material, goes in the belly and is cast out. But it becomes beneficial, and gives the mind insight to apprehend that which truly benefits us, according to the prayer that supervenes upon it and the proportion of faith. Not the material bread, but the word said over it, benefits the worthy eater.

[75] *str.* 1. 19. 96.
[76] *paed.* 2. 2. 19, 20.
[77] *Jo.* 32. 24.
[78] *eccl. theol.* 3. 12.
[79] "Basil". *ep.* 8. 4.
[80] *Cels.* 8. 33.

All this relates to the typical and symbolical body; but the Word has become flesh, and is true food. The eater of this will live for ever, but no wicked person can ever eat of it.[81]

Athanasius may be thinking on rather similar lines when he carefully distinguishes in John 6 between the visible flesh of Christ and the spirit and life which he promises as the food of believers.[82] In the fourth century, however, there is an increasing tendency to speak of a "change" of the elements, by consecration, into the body and blood of Christ. This often co-exists with a continued use of the language of symbolism. Cyril of Jerusalem, who may be said to introduce this conception, compares the change with the miracle of Cana; but he continues: "in the figure (τύπος) of bread the body is given . . . so that receiving Christ's body you may become 'concorporate (σύσσωμος) with him",[83] (an idea which has highly important implications in the later Christological controversies). Jerome,[84] and Ambrose,[85] who certainly stands in Cyril's tradition, also continue to use the language of symbolism.

The idea of "change" had already been expressed by Theodotus the Valentinian; not as substantial, but as "dynamic". Bread, and oil (probably for chrismation (cf. Cyril of Jerusalem, *catech.* 21. 3), are changed by divine δύναμις into spiritual δύναμις, and this also happens to baptismal water.[86] The word used here is μεταβάλλεσθαι employed frequently from Cyril of Jerusalem onwards to describe the "conversion" of the elements.[87] Similar terms include μεταποιεῖσθαι,[88] μεταρρυθμίζεσθαι,[89] μεταστοιχειοῦσθαι.[90] This is held to be effected, not now through the prayer of thanksgiving itself but rather through the supervention or illapse of the Logos, as in Sarapion's anaphora[91] (this is to be distinguished from Irenaeus'

---

81 *comm. in Mt.* 11. 14.
82 *ep. Sarap.* 4. 19.
83 *catech.* 22. 2, 3.
84 *Jer.* 3. 10.
85 *sacr.* 4. 21; 6. 3.
86 *Clem. exc. Thdt.* 82.
87 E.g., Cyril of Jerusalem, *catech.* 23-7; Theodore of Mopsuestia, *Mt.* 26. 26; Cyril of Alexandria, *ep. Calos..* 365B; Theodoret, *eran.* 1, 2 (Schulze 4. 26, 126).
88 Gregory of Nyssa, *or. catech.* 37; cf. Ambrose cited by Theodoret, *eran.* 2 (4. 145).
89 Chrysostom, *prod. Jud.* 2. 6.
90 Gregory of Nyssa, loc. cit., and others.
91 15.

"bread receives the word of God",[92] which probably refers to the words of Institution which he has just mentioned), or of the Spirit, in response to the prayer of invocation (ἐπίκλησις), as in the *Didascalia* (*gratiarum actio* (i.e., εὐχαριστία) *per Spiritum sanctum sanctificatur*),[93] Cyril of Jerusalem,[94] the Liturgy of the *Apostolic Constitutions*[95] (the Spirit is prayed for "to show forth this bread as Christ's body"), and Chrysostom.[96] Equally, and with no sense of contradiction, the conversion may be attributed to the recitation of the words of Institution, the creative word of Christ, as it is by Gregory of Nyssa,[97] Chrysostom,[98] and Ambrose.[99] The theory of conversion is developed in answer to the question *how* bread and wine can *be* Christ's body and blood, (for example, by Cyril of Jerusalem, Theodore, and Ambrose); and in turn it gives rise to the question how the one and entire body of Christ can be received daily without suffering division. The reply given by Gregory of Nyssa is that the bread and wine are taken up into the body of Christ by a transformation of their elementary nature (μεταστοιχειοῦν) so as to *become* that body.[100] Such a "conversionist" doctrine is accompanied by a tendency for the Eucharist to lose something of its early character of a joyful celebration of thanksgiving and eschatological hope, and to become an occasion when the "dread" and "awful" sacrifice is set forth. Such epithets as these are characteristic of Chrysostom and many other writers of the fourth century and later, and they are accompanied by a growing insistence on the danger of Communion for the unworthy. It also naturally goes along with a strong insistence that the eucharistic body is the actual flesh of Christ's earthly life, and the eucharistic blood that which was shed at Calvary,[101] though Ambrose is careful to point out that the body of Christ is spiritual

---

92 *haer.* 5. 2. 3.
93 6. 21. 2.
94 *catech.* 23. 7.
95 8. 12. 39.
96 *sac.* 3. 4.
97 Gregory of Nyssa, loc. cit.
98 *prod. Jud.* 1. 6.
99 *myst.* 9 .54; *sacr.* 4. 4. 14. 15.
100 Gregory of Nyssa, loc. cit.
101 E.g., Chrysostom, *hom.* 24 1ff. *in 1 Cor.*; Ambrose, *myst.* 9. 53.

and not corporeal food; the body of Christ is the body of the Spirit, since the Spirit is Christ (Lam. 4. 20).[102]

Professor H. Chadwick has shown[103] how closely the Christology of Cyril of Alexandria is determined by the conviction that in the Eucharist it is the life-giving flesh of the divine Logos that is received.[104] He objects to the traditional "symbolism": "Christ did not say that the things seen are a figure (τύπος), but that the elements are transformed (μεταποιεῖσθαι) into his body and blood"[105] (an objection which was shared by Theodore of Mopsuestia[106]), and he finds in Nestorius' teaching the dangerous implication that the eucharistic flesh is that of a man, not the Logos, and hence that it cannot be life-giving and deifying.[107] Nestorius himself is equally concerned with the reality of the eucharistic participation in Christ's flesh; but for him it is essential to safeguard the truth, which he believed Cyril to deny, that this is consubstantial with our flesh, so that it may truly be a means by which we are assured of resurrection.[108] The "two natures" Christology, however, asserting the distinct reality of the divinity and the humanity in Christ's Person without "confusion", had as its natural counterpart a eucharistic doctrine which distinguished sharply between the sign and the thing signified. Theodoret makes the point at length in his anti-monophysite argument: the language of "conversion" must be avoided; in the words of Institution "our Saviour exchanged the names, and gave to the body the name of the symbol, and to the symbol that of the body . . . He did not change (μεταβάλλειν) the nature of the elements but added grace to their nature"; and, alluding to Hebrews 10. 5, he remarks: "It does not say, 'Thou hast converted (μεταβάλλειν) into a body; but, 'A body hast thou prepared for me' ".[109]

The later Greek theologians, however, show an increasing dislike of this dichotomy. John of Damascus is typical. God, he says, uses ordinary objects to produce what is supernatural. His creative

102 Ambrose, *myst.* 9. 58.
103 *JTS* (Ns) II, pp. 145-64.
104 E.g., *Lc.* 22. 19, *glaph. in Ex.* (*PG* LXIX. 428A).
105 *Mt.* 26. 26.
106 *catech.* 6; *Mt.* loc. cit.
107 *Nest.* 4. 5, 6, etc.
108 *Heracl.* 39-49.
109 *eran.* 1 (4. 26).

word makes bread his body, and wine and water his blood, by the invocation and supervention of the Spirit. There is no question of the ascended body coming down, but of bread and wine being changed into God's body and blood, so as to be no more two realities but one and the same. They are not a figure (τύπος) of body and blood (God forbid!), but the actual body of the Lord. As in the hypostatic union in Christ, there is a union of two natures, of bread and of deity, typified by Isaiah's coal which was wood united with fire. The elements may be called "antitypes", as they were by Basil, but only before they are consecrated. It is, however, proper to call them figures ("antitypes") of things to come, not in the sense that they are not truly the body and blood, but because now we participate through them in Christ's deity whereas hereafter we shall do so by immediate apprehension.[110]

In the West, Ambrose, while not eschewing the "symbolist" terminolgy, follows this Eastern pattern of thought. The sacraments (i.e., the elements) are transformed (*transfigurare*) by the mystery of the holy prayer into flesh and blood.[111] If the word of Elijah, he asks, could alter the course of nature, shall not Christ's word be able to change the character (*species*) of the elements? It could create out of nothing that which was not, and therefore can change things which are into that which they were not. It is not a lesser act to give new natures to things (i.e., in creation) than to change their natures.[112]

Augustine, on the other hand, continues to maintain a very plain distinction between outward sign and inward reality; he also recognizes that the sacrament is one among many means of communion with Christ. Our daily bread is the sacrament of the altar; it is also the preached word, readings, and hymns. The virtue, or effect, of the Eucharist is unity, so that, being made members of Christ's body, we may be that which we receive.[113] Our eyes see bread and the cup; to faith they are Christ's body and blood. They are sacraments, because in them one thing is seen and another is understood. What is placed on the altar is the mystery of ourselves: one bread, made of many grains. "Be what you are see, and receive what you are".

110 *fid. orth.* 4. 13.
111 *fid* 4. 10. 124.
112 *myst.* 9. 52.
113 *serm.* 59. 6; 57. 7

Wine is made from many grapes: the mystery of unity requires the maintenance of the bond of peace.[114] To eat Christ's flesh does not mean that his body, which ascended entire, is consumed; it is to eat and drink unfailing life. What is received visibly must in actual reality be eaten and drunk spiritually.[115] The bread is Christ: "prepare you heart, not your throat; it is not what is seen but what is believed that feeds us".[116] In eating the manna, Israel received the *same* spiritual food that we take.[117] What Christ gave to the disciples at the Supper was a *figura* of his body and blood.[118] In John 6 the crowds took the words of Jesus literally; but "the flesh profits you nothing" means that they must be understood spiritually: "you are not going to eat this body that you see, nor drink the blood that those who crucify him will shed". Christ has given us a sacrament; although it has to be celebrated visibly, it must be invisibly understood;[119] for any biblical precept which seems to order evil to be done is figurative, and John 6. 54 is therefore a figure, bidding us to communicate in the Lord's passion and store up beneficially in our memory that for us his flesh was crucified.[120]

This teaching, with its strong refusal to confuse the sign with the thing signified, is not at variance with Augustine's curious statement that, "when Christ said 'This is my body', he carried his body in his hands". The passage is a *tour-de-force* of exegesis. In the Old Latin text of the story of David and Achish, David feigned madness and "was carried in his hands" (*ferebatur in manibus suis*; AV, "he scrabbled with his hands"). Augustine applies this unpromising text to John 6. When Christ's words (John 6. 54) were taken literally by the crowd, he seemed to be mad; but at the Institution his body was carried in his hands. This however, was not done literally but *quodam modo* (i.e., in a sacrament).[121]

Augustine's position is the basis of the doctrine of Rabanus Maurus and Ratramn. The differences between the latter and Radbert sometimes give an appearance of obscurity, because they

114 *serm.* 272.
115 *serm.* 131. 1.
116 *serm.* 112. 4, 5.
117 *serm.* 352. 3.
118 *enarr. in Ps.* 3. 1.
119 *enarr. in Ps.* 98. 9.
120 *doct. Christ.* 3. 24.
121 *enarr.* 1 *in Ps.* 33. 8, 10; *enarr.* 2 *in Ps.* 33. 2.

are hampered by their lack of an agreed technical vocabulary. Ratramn's point, however, is clear; the inward and heavenly gift and the external sign, figure, or sacrament of bread and wine are both real entities. The distinct entity of the elements is not absorbed or changed into the body and blood which are spiritually received. Radbert, on the other hand, acknowledges that the figure or sign of bread and wine persists after consecration; but for him this is not a separate entity but simply the external appearance of what has become a single reality by conversion. He is arguing for what is practically a transubstantiationist view, but he lacks the precise terminology of substance and accidents.

Ratramn argues that the faithful receive the body and blood in a mystery; what appears to the senses is one thing, what faith apprehends is another. In a figure one thing is said, another is indicated. That Christ was born or suffered is a literal statement; "I am the living bread", or "I am the vine", is not, for Christ is not substantially bread nor a vine. This does not mean that Ratramn denies the true presence of Christ in the Eucharist or that he thinks, as Berengar was accused by Lanfranc of believing, that the sacrament is merely an aid to recollection. What is received is Christ's body, made such by the priest's ministry. But outwardly it is one thing, displaying the properties of bread, while another, the divine reality, is not received bodily but by the insight of the believing mind. Literalists, he says, ought either to deny that the elements are body and blood or to acknowledge that the change is spiritual: spiritual body and blood existing under the veil of corporeal bread and wine. The Eucharist is parallel to Baptism: in the latter the virtue of the Spirit supervenes on material water, as such capable only of cleansing the body, and makes it efficacious to wash the soul; in the former, bread and wine, capable only of feeding the body, are changed spiritually by divine *virtus* into the efficacious mystery of Christ's body and blood. It is the operation of the Spirit which gives life. Bread and wine are Christ's body and blood because they minister the substance of eternal life.

Ratramn also makes use of the ancient symbolism of the water in the mixed cup, signifying the people of Christ. A literalist interpretation of consecration would mean that this is converted into the people's blood; hence the identification of the water with the Church must, of course, be understood spiritually. The same applies to the relation of the wine to the blood of Christ. The bread, too, is a mystery both of Christ's body and of the body of his people. The body in which Christ suffered and the body which is a memorial of his Passion are not the same entity. All this does not mean that the faithful do not really receive Christ's body and blood. Faith does receive it, as spiritual food and drink.[122]

Radbert, in the "conversionist" tradition of the East and of Ambrose, maintains that the consecrated elements *are* in reality (*veritas*) that which was born of Mary, died and rose, though they are received in a sacrament by faith and the outward aspect is not changed; for we walk by faith, not sight. The sacrament is at the same time *figura* and *veritas*; not a figure or type which points to a reality different from itself, as the manna was, but a figure which is the external appearance of the inner *veritas*. What we receive is entirely *veritas*, whereas the manna was not the angels' food in *re*, but in *specie et figura*. The substance of bread and wine is inwardly changed into Christ's flesh and blood, received by the faithful from the heavenly altar to which the priest prays that the elements may be conveyed to the angel. To the worthy it brings spiritual food, to the unworthy judgement. We receive Christ's flesh. It could not be more real if the colour and taste of bread were changed. This does not happen, for, if it did, meritorious faith would not be required, nor could the mystery be concealed from unbelievers. Radbert, however, again cites stories, mainly from Gregory the Great, to show that there have been frequent revelations of the consecrated elements in the form of a lamb or with the colour of flesh and blood. Though the elements may continue to be called bread and wine, as being the bread of life and the wine that gladdens the heart of the inner man, they are nothing else than Christ's body and blood.[123]

This extreme realism opens the way for Berengar's objection to "conversionism". Either the bread is taken up to heaven, there to be transformed into Christ's flesh, or Christ's flesh is brought down to earth for the bread to be changed into it there. Neither happens. Therefore the bread is not converted into true flesh.[124] Lanfranc's

---

122 The above is a summary of the main arguments of Ratramn, *de corp. et sang. Dom. (PL* CXXI. 125ff).
123 Radbert, *de corp. et sang. Dom. (PL* CXX. 1257ff.).
124 Lanfranc, *de sacr. corp. et sang. Christi* xxi.

only answer is, in effect, that Berengar ought to pray either for understanding or else for faith in that which lies beyond the bounds of reason. He counter-attacks by claiming that Berengar taught that the elements after consecration remain what they were, and are called Christ's flesh and blood only because they are "celebrated" in memory of the crucified flesh and the poured-out blood, so that we may remember the passion and be moved to crucify the flesh with its lusts (an interpretation of his views which is not borne out by Berengar's later *de Sacra Coena*, according to which the body of Christ in heaven is given to the faithful on earth through the effective sign or figure of bread and wine). Lanfranc then asserts that this doctrine makes the Christian sacrament inferior to the manna and to the Old Testament sacrifices.[125] For the rest, the controversy between Lanfranc and Berengar turns largely on the exegesis of Augustine and other Fathers.

How far eucharistic theory has really moved from the patristic teaching is indicated by the confession imposed on Berengar by Nicholas II's council of 1059: "Bread and wine which are placed on the altar are, after consecration, not only a sacrament but also the true body and blood of our Lord, and are sensibly, not only in a sacrament but in reality, handled by the priests, broken, and crushed by the teeth of the faithful".

[125] Ibid., 22.

4

THE EUCHARIST IN
THE REFORMATION ERA

C. W. DUGMORE

THE theological and philosophical background to the eucharistic controversies of the period of the sixteenth-century Reformation and Counter-Reformation are necessarily different from those of the "Patristic Period", even if the latter period is extended to include the eleventh-century writer, Berengar, to whom many of the Reformers appealed as to one of the Fathers of the Church. Scholasticism—Thomism, Scotism, the Nominalism of William of Ockham and the followers of the *Devotio Moderna*—had intervened. Thus, all the early Reformers were brought up in the tradition of late medieval theology and philosophy. Luther, for example, having proceeded B.A. in 1502 and M.A. in 1505 at the University of Erfurt through the usual course, the *trivium* (grammar, logic and rhetoric) and the *quadrivium* (geometry, mathematics, music and astronomy) and the natural, metaphysical, and moral philosophy of Aristotle, studied, in the course of his preparation for ordination in 1507, the *Canonis Misse Expositio*,[1] based on a course of eighty-nine lectures by Gabriel Biel (c. 1420-95), the nominalist professor of theology in the new University of Tübingen, which he delivered in the years between 1484 and 1488. This work was also studied by Cranmer and by John Jewel later, both of whom read theology and not law—as most of the statesmen-bishops of an earlier generation had done. It is, therefore, important to view the doctrinal disputes of the six-

---

[1] *Gabrielis Biel Canonis Misse Expositio*, ed. Heiko A. Oberman and W. J. Courtenay (Veröffentlichungen des Instituts für europäische Geschichte Mainz 31, 32), i (1963), ii (1965), to be published in 4 vols. by Franz Steiner (Wiesbaden).

teenth century as a continuation of the theological debates of the
Middle Ages. New influences were at work and new ideas were
abroad, but essentially as Christian thinkers the Reformers were
facing the same questions as the Schoolmen and were engaged in the
same search for ultimate truth.

1 THE EUCHARISTIC SACRIFICE

That the Eucharist is a sacrifice connected with the passion as well
as with the heavenly life of our Lord was a tradition inherited by
the early Middle Ages from Augustine and Gregory the Great. The
ninth and eleventh centuries witnessed the great eucharistic controversies concerning the presence of Christ in the sacrament associated
with the names of Paschasius Radbertus/Ratramnus and Lanfranc/
Berengar. But these theologians were not unconcerned with the
doctrine of the sacrifice of the Mass. Thus, Paschasius declared, "We
continually reproduce the memory of his most holy death by daily
offering the sacrifice of his most sacred body and blood on the
altar" (*de corp. et sang. dom.*, ix. 2; *PL*, cxx. 1295 A). Notice the
word, "*memory*". Does he believe that there is a daily repetition
in the Mass of the sacrifice offered by Christ on Calvary? He says,
"because we daily fall, Christ is daily immolated for us mystically
(*quotidie pro nobis Christus mystice immolatur*)" (ibid., ix. 1; *PL*,
cxx. 1294 A); "he daily takes away the sins of the world . . . when
the commemoration of his blessed passion is reproduced at the altar
(*cum eiusdem beatae passionis ad altare memoria replicatur*)" (ibid.,
ix. 2; *PL* cxx. 1294 C). Thus, Paschasius regarded the daily offering
of the sacrifice as a memorial (ἀνάμνησις) of the passion, though he
spoke of it also as a mystical immolation.

Alger of Liège (1070–*c.* 1131) was careful to insist that there is
no fresh immolation in the Mass distinct from that upon the cross
(*de sacramento*, xvi : *PL*, clxxx. 786), but he held that Christ is
daily mystically immolated for us in the unbloody sacrifice of the
Mass (ibid., 788). This was the tradition inherited by Peter Lombard,
Thomas Aquinas, and the later Schoolmen, including Gabriel Biel.
It was accepted by Luther and is implicitly accepted by the Catechism of the Book of Common Prayer which asserts that the sacrament of the Lord's Supper was instituted as "the continual
remembrance of the sacrifice of the death of Christ and of the
benefits which we receive thereby".

Professor E. L. Mascall, following the late Dr Hicks,[2] has argued that discussion of the eucharistic sacrifice since the sixteenth century has "been dominated by the medieval conception of sacrifice as consisting exclusively in the death of the victim, this being taken in complete isolation from the circumstances which led up to it, accompanied it or followed from it".[3] He has, therefore, seen what he calls the "Reformation Deadlock" in the Catholic insistence that the Eucharist is a repetition of Calvary and the Protestant insistence that it is a commemoration of Calvary—even though he concedes that Catholics have generally asserted that it is not a *literal* repetition and Protestants that it is not a *bare* commemoration. All this follows, according to Mascall, from the mistaken medieval identification of sacrifice with mactation, the idea that sacrifice, immolation, involves necessarily the death of the victim. It would seem, however, that this is an over-simplification of the facts and that Dr Mascall has fallen into the very error which he accuses the Protestant Reformers of having fallen into. Father Francis Clark, S.J., has produced a catena of extracts from the leading Catholic apologists of the early Reformation period in order to show that "the so-called 'medieval equation' proves to be a misnomer".[4] He holds that the equation sacrifice = death, in the sense that the eucharistic sacrifice = a new putting to death of Christ, is an equation that was imagined not by the medieval theologians but by Zwingli in 1523 ("as if any victim can be slain before God without also being offered to him, or offered without being slain").[5] Calvin certainly denied that there could be such a thing as an "unbloody sacrifice" (*Institutes*, IV. xviii. 5). Father Clark tries to prove that Luther did not imagine that the papists believed in some kind of new slaying of Christ in every Mass, but that he merely objected to the notion of the sacrifice of the Mass as a "good work" and because it derogated from Christ's sacrifice once offered upon Calvary. Nevertheless, the passage from Luther

2 F. C. N. Hicks, *The Fullness of Sacrifice*, London, 1930; 3rd edn, 1946; cf. B. J. Kidd, *The Later Medieval Doctrine of the Eucharistic Sacrifice*, London, 1898, reissued 1958.

3 E. L. Mascall, *Corpus Christi*, London 1953, p. 82, 2nd edn 1965, p. 107.

4 Francis Clark, S.J., *Eucharistic Sacrifice and the Reformation*, London, 1960, pp. 391-3, 401.

5 Cited by Clark, op. cit., p. 395; cf. the passages cited from other Reformers who are alleged to have adopted Zwingli's argument (ibid., pp. 396ff).

quoted by Father Clark (p. 397) ends with the words, "In truth your re-sacrificing is a most impious re-crucifying"—which rather militates against Clark. Clearly, Luther *did* think the papists believed in some kind of new slaying of Christ in every Mass.

In the second edition of his book *Corpus Christi* (1965) Dr Mascall has conceded that his suggestion that, because of their identification of sacrifice with death, Catholics thought of the Mass in terms of repetition of Calvary and Protestants in terms of commemoration "may need revision" in the light of Father Clark's discussion. He is less approving of the eucharistic theology of St Thomas Aquinas than is Anthony A. Stephenson, [who wrote "Two Views of the Mass: Medieval Linguistic Abuses"[6] when still a Jesuit (he is now an Anglican)], though he does not question Stephenson's insistence that the Angelic Doctor, whilst employing the dangerously ambiguous traditional language, emphasized that "Christ is *not* actually immolated (slain) in the Mass, and that the Mass is *not* (in the obvious sense of the phrase) the same sacrifice as Calvary".[7] Stephenson goes on to point out that in the course of the Middle Ages St Thomas's theology of the Mass underwent a subtle transformation, so that the theory of representation of Calvary became a theory of *re*-presentation—which, "Father Clark tells us, was actually one of the two dominant theories of the Mass in the Late Middle Ages (op. cit., pp. 264-5) . . . This theory, therefore, clearly teaches that in the Mass Christ is, quite literally, crucified, that in the Mass there is a 'bloody mactation'. This theory of the liberal identity of the Mass and the cross does not, of course, teach a *new* slaying of Christ; nevertheless . . . it would be extremely difficult to make the less-educated faithful grasp and remember the subtle distinction between the numerical identity of the Mass and the cross, which the theory asserts, and a specific identity, which would make the Mass a *repetition* of Calvary".[8]

It appears, therefore, that while Dr Mascall is too categorical in his insistence on "the medieval equation", Father Clark, on the other hand, contradicts himself in his otherwise valuable book by first attributing the equation to Zwingli and his successors and then admitting that the *re*-presentation theory, involving the identity

[6] In *Theological Studies*, xxii (1961), pp. 588-609.
[7] Ibid., p. 599.
[8] Ibid., pp. 604-5.

of the sacrifice of the cross and that of the altar, was one of the two dominant theories of the Mass in the later Middle Ages. Certainly in popular belief this identification involved stories of bleeding hosts, and the repetition of Calvary in every Mass is assumed in Mirk's *Instruction for Parish Priests* and in his *Festial*: "so yet each day in the Mass he sheddeth his blood in high meed to all that this believe".[9] Father Clark (op. cit., pp. 426-9) argues that all these instances refer to the real presence and not to the sacrifice of the Mass. But this will not do. It is impossible to separate the two things, except in abstract theological discussion. As Clark himself remarked earlier (op. cit., p. 264), the whole notion of the eucharistic sacrifice takes on a different meaning according to whether the doctrine of the real objective presence of Christ in the consecrated elements is admitted or denied.

Among the theologians it is doubtless true that a distinction *was* made between the bloody sacrifice once offered upon the cross and the unbloody representation of that sacrifice in the Mass. Thus Gabriel Biel, whilst asserting that the Mass is a true sacrifice since the same victim is daily offered up, yet emphasized that the offering of the Mass is not a reiteration, but a representation, of the offering on the cross, to call forth the mercy of God.[10] It would, however, be wrong to imagine that for Biel the Eucharist is "a 'mere memorial', a psychological representation of a past historical event. The *repraesentatio* of Calvary means participation in the inheritance disclosed in the testament signed by the blood of Christ on Calvary".[11]

For Zwingli the Lord's Supper was a "mere memorial", but both he and his successor Bullinger laid stress on the idea of the testament signed by the blood of Christ, the new law, and the promise "whose office is to lead us to Christ by the right way of faith, which faith makes us partakers of Christ". So, while the Zwinglians rejected all notions of sacrifice other than that of Christ on the cross, of the *repraesentatio* of Calvary in the Eucharist, they

9 See further, C. W. Dugmore, *The Mass and the English Reformers*, London, 1958, pp. 76-8.
10 See the passages cited in Heiko A. Oberman, *The Harvest of Medieval Theology*, Harvard, 1963, 273; cf. his *Forerunners of the Reformation*, London, 1967, 248-9.
11 Oberman, *Harvest*, 275.

shared with Gabriel Biel the belief that the efficacy of the sacrament lies in the testament referred to by Christ in the words of
institution and personal faith in the promise. Luther violently
repudiated what he believed to be the medieval doctrine of the
Mass as a sacrifice and a *bonum opus*. Like Zwingli he inherited
from Biel the testament-idea and regarded the Eucharist as a
memorial or commemoration of the sacrifice of the cross rather
than a repetition or representation of it. But Luther had a keen
sense of the mystery of the sacrament, which was almost entirely
lacking in Zwingli, and he stressed the mystical communion-fellowship of the worthy communicants united with Christ in the self-
oblation of the Church. Calvin, too, while rejecting any notion of
repetition of the atoning sacrifice of Christ which would derogate
from the merits of Christ, put the element of mystery at the centre
of his teaching and, since for him the ultimate meaning of the
Eucharist is union with the continually present Saviour whose glorified body is in heaven and not in the elements, though "the reality
is joined to them [the signs]",[12] the only possible sacrificial offering
in the Eucharist is the sacrifice of praise and thanksgiving, "and
commemoration for the flesh of Christ which he offered and for
the blood which he poured out for the remission of our sins".[13]
Thanksgiving and commemoration, and Communion are the purposes for which the Lord's Supper was instituted. Christ by his
unique sacrifice satisfied the wrath of God, procured for us perpetual righteousness and "is entered into the heavenly sanctuary,
finally to appear for us, and intercede with the virtue of his
sacrifice".[14]

Similarly, in the Communion Office of the English Prayer Book
of 1549 the emphasis was upon the anamnesis of the passion, resurrection and ascension of Christ, Communion, the "sacrifice of
praise and thanksgiving" and the self-oblation of the Church. The
ancient Canon of the Mass was altered so as to exclude the belief
that the Eucharist was itself an oblation actually being offered at
the altar, and the "offertory" became simply a collection of alms.

[12] Calvin, *Short Treatise on the Holy Supper of our Lord and only Saviour
Jesus Christ*, in *Calvin: Theological Treatises*, ed. J. K. S. Reid (Library of
Christian Classics, xxii), London, 1954, p. 166.
[13] Reid, op. cit., p. 42.
[14] Read, op. cit., pp. 162-3.

2 THE REAL PRESENCE

The changes effected in the liturgies of the sixteenth century with regard to the eucharistic sacrifice and the manner in which the Reformers spoke of it were partly due to their desire to avoid any confusion in the minds of ordinary Christians between the sacrifice of the altar and the sacrifice of the cross, which they all regarded as the "one oblation once offered, a full, perfect, and sufficient sacrifice, oblation, and satisfaction for the sins of the whole world". They were also due to the universal rejection of the doctrine of transubstantiation by the Reformers, both on the Continent and in England.

The statement issued by the Fourth Lateran Council of 1215, that Christ's "body and blood are really contained in the sacrament of the altar under the species of bread and wine, the bread being transubstantiated into the body and the wine into the blood by the power of God", afforded no explicit definition as to the change of substance or the retention of the accidents, or, indeed, as to the nature of the presence. These and other questions arising from them occupied the attention of the scholastic theologians from Bonaventura, Thomas Aquinas, and Duns Scotus to William of Ockham and Gabriel Biel. The debate was continued in the sixteenth century, both between Catholics and Protestants and between the Protestant leaders themselves. For, until the Council of Trent officially defined the teaching of the Roman Church on the subject in its sessions of 1551 and 1552, there was no single official interpretation in existence. The *Catechism of the Council of Trent* embodying the doctrines approved at the Council was not issued until 1566.

It is impossible here to enter into a detailed discussion of scholastic philosophy and theology as it affects the mode of Christ's presence in the Eucharist. Most of the scholastic philosophers held that quantity is a reality distinct from substance and quality. They agreed on the fact that Christ is present with his quantity in the Eucharist—i.e., the totality is present—but not through his quantity as he is in heaven. Thus Duns Scotus admitted the reality of quantity, but Ockham did not think of quantity as an entity separate from substance and quality: for him quantity was "a connotative term which signifies either a substance or a quality".[15] Biel sided

15 Gabriel Buescher, *The Eucharistic Teaching of William of Ockham*, St Bonaventure, 1950, p. 67.

with Ockham as against Duns Scotus on this question, but, like Ockham, "Biel defines the real presence of Christ in the Eucharist in such a way that the historical body of Christ, the issue of the Virgin Mary, becomes present on the altar".[16] He utterly rejected the figurative meaning of the words, "This is my body".

The dispute between Luther and Zwingli which culminated at the Colloquy of Marburg in 1529 was, as everyone knows, concerned with this very question. Luther followed Biel in asserting the real presence of Christ on the altar (though not by transubstantiation), while Zwingli held to the figurative sense, viz., that *est = significat*. In the final resort their wholly different understandings of the eucharistic presence were due to their different conceptions of God. Zwingli's rationalism and his emphasis on the transcendence of God resulted in a local conception of heaven (where Christ now sits at God's right hand) and left no place in his eucharistic doctrine for the element of mystery. It is through communion-fellowship that we express our thanksgiving for Christ's self-offering upon the cross, and those who eat the bread and drink the cup proclaim Christ's death, confess that they are members of his Church, and by their faith are incorporated into the body of Christ. Luther also stressed in his early writings the idea of communion-fellowship, which goes back, of course, to St Augustine and to St Paul. But he combined with it the mystery of the forgiveness of sins and of God's grace given in the sacrament through the objective real presence of the body and blood of Christ. In his *Sermon von dem Sakrament des Leibes und Blutes Christi* (1526) he wrote, "God is everywhere, but he does not desire that you should seek everywhere but only where the Word is. There if you will seek him you will truly find, namely in the Word. These people do not know and see who say that it does not make sense that Christ should be in bread and wine. Of course Christ is with me in prison and the martyr's death, else where should I be? He is truly present there with the Word, yet not in the same sense as in the sacrament, because he has attached his body and blood to the Word and in bread and wine is bodily to be received".[17] In his

---

[16] Oberman, *Harvest*, pp. 275-6.

[17] *Works*, Weimar edn, xix. p. 492 cited by Roland Bainton, *Here I Stand*, New York, 1950, p. 224; cf. Y. Brilioth, *Eucharistic Faith and Practice Evangelical and Catholic*, London, 1930, p. 104.

desire to correct the local conception of the Divine Being, Luther insisted upon God's omnipresence and so evolved the doctrine of the ubiquity of Christ's presence which is one of his most characteristic ideas.

St Thomas had declared that "the dimensions of the bread and wine are not changed into the dimensions of the body of Christ, but substance into substance. And so the substance of Christ's body or blood is under this sacrament by the power of the sacrament, but not the dimensions of Christ's body or blood. Hence it is clear that the body of Christ is in the sacrament by way of substance, and not by way of quantity" (*ST*, iii. 76, art. 1 ad. 3). Duns Scotus and William of Ockham replaced Aquinas's "dimensive quantity" by "quality". Following Ockham, Gabriel Biel held that "while the body of Christ exists *circumscriptive* [the usual mode of local presence of a thing, as of wine in a jar] in heaven, it is present on the altar *definitive* [as the presence of the soul in the body or an angel in a certain place]; in heaven Christ leads a quantitative existence, on the altar not".[18] In his doctrine of ubiquity Luther carried this teaching to its logical conclusion : "We hold that the body of Christ must not be in one place only locally, that is, by way of dimensions, but we hold that the body of Christ can also be at the same time in other ways in more places than one . . . and it is not true that the body of Christ cannot be in any other way than locally, that is, by way of dimensions." It can, therefore, be at the same time in more places than one—in heaven and sacramentally in innumerable Eucharists.

But Luther held that the sacramental presence is limited to the time of the administration of the sacrament. Lengthy discussions occur in the writings of Alexander of Hales, Albertus Magnus, Bonaventura, Aquinas, and other doctors as to the precise "moment of consecration". Luther dismissed all these quibbles. "We will define the time or sacramental action," he wrote, "as beginning from the beginning of the Lord's Prayer, and lasting until all have communicated and they have emptied the cup and consumed the particles and the people have been dismissed and the departure from

---

18 Cited in Oberman, *Harvest*, p. 276.

the altar has taken place. So we shall be safe and free from the scruples and scandals of endless questions".[19]

Thomas Cranmer did not share Luther's ideas about the ubiquity of Christ's body although he, too, believed that "Christ's flesh and blood be in the sacrament truly present, but spiritually and sacramentally, not carnally and corporally. And as he is truly present, so is he truly eaten and drunken, and assisteth us".[20] In his *Answer* to Stephen Gardiner he clearly repudiated the charge of holding a Zwinglian, or sacramentarian, view of the Eucharist: "And therefore I never said of the whole supper, that it is but a signification or a bare memory of Christ's death; but I teach that it is a spiritual refreshing, wherein our souls be fed and nourished with Christ's very flesh and blood to eternal life. And therefore bring you forth some place in my book [*A Defence of the True and Catholic Doctrine of the Sacrament of the Body and Blood of our Saviour Christ*], where I say that the Lord's supper is but a bare signification without any effect or operation of God in the same".[21] On the contrary, "unto the faithful Christ is at his own holy table present, with his mighty Spirit and grace, and is of them more fruitfully received, than if corporally they should receive him bodily present".[22] The unworthy eat and drink to their own damnation, "because they do not duly consider Christ's very flesh and blood, which be offered there spiritually to be eaten and drunken".[23] This is neither Zwinglian nor Lutheran doctrine: it is Cranmerian, and it has at least as long a pedigree as Luther's doctrine.[24]

However, Cranmer does seem to have been at one with Luther in regard to the "ministration of the sacrament". We quoted above Luther's definition of the sacramental action as beginning with the Lord's Prayer (which preceeded the Communion) and "lasting until all have communicated . . . and the people have been dismissed". Similarly Cranmer in his Preface to the *Answer:* "by this word 'sacrament' I mean the whole ministration and receiving

---

[19] Letter of 20 July 1543, cited in Darwell Stone, *A History of the Doctrine of the Holy Eucharist*, London, 1909, 2. p. 24.

[20] Cranmer, *Works*, ed. Parker Society, i. p. 87.

[21] Op. cit., p. 148.

[22] Op. cit., p. 219.

[23] Ibid.

[24] See Dugmore, op. cit.

of the sacraments . . . in the due ministration of the sacraments according to Christ's ordinance and institution, Christ and his holy Spirit be truly and indeed present by their mighty and sanctifying power, virtue, and grace, in all them that worthily receive the same".[25]

Professor E. C. Ratcliff, in the course of a most illuminating article in *Theology*[26] on the subject of the theory of consecration in England quoted the well-known passage from Cranmer's *Defence* which begins with the definition : "Consecration is the separation of any thing from a profane and worldly use unto a spiritual and godly use," and goes on, with reference to the Eucharist, "but specially they may be called holy and consecrated when they be separated to that holy use by Christ's own words, which he spake for that purpose, saying of the bread, *This is my body;* and of the wine, *This is my blood.* So that commonly the authors [the patristic writers], before those words be spoken, do take the bread and wine but as other bread and wine; but after those words be pronounced over them, then they take them for consecrated and holy bread and wine. Not that the bread and wine can be partakers of any holiness or godliness, or can be the body and blood of Christ; but that they represent [? re-present] the very body and blood of Christ, and the holy food and nourishment which we have by him. And so they be called by the names of the body and blood of Christ." Ratcliff's only other quotation from Cranmer (and again from the *Defence*) was a passage cited from St John Damascene to much the same effect. In this section of the *Defence*, however, Cranmer was primarily concerned with arguing against the papist doctrine of transubstantiation. Thus he quotes with approval Eusebius Emissenus as to "how the bread and wine be converted into the body and blood of Christ and yet remain still in their nature"[27] and Augustine : "as the person of Christ consisteth of two natures, that is to say of his manhood and of his Godhead, and therefore both those natures remain in Christ; even so, saith St Augustine, the sacrament con-

---

25 *Works*, P.S., i. 3.
26 E. C. Ratcliff, "The English Usage of Eucharistic Consecration 1548-1662", in *Theology*, LX (1957), pp. 229-36, 273-80. The writer does not share Professor Ratcliff's interpretation of Cranmer's eucharistic doctrine and, therefore, does not accept his view that Cranmer's theory of consecration differed from Jewel's.
27 Cranmer, *Remains*, ed. H. Jenkyns, Oxford, 1833. ii, p. 323.

sisteth of two natures, of the elements of bread and wine, and of
the body and blood of Christ, and therefore both these natures must
remain in the sacrament."[28] In his *Answer* Cranmer tried to make
clearer his understanding of the passage in Emissenus: "he speaketh
not of any real and corporal conversion . . . nor of any corporal and
real eating and drinking . . .: but he speaketh of a sacramental
conversion of bread and wine, and of a spiritual eating and drinking
of the body and blood."[29]

It is clear from this passage, and from others which might be cited,
that Cranmer distinguished between the "sacramental conversion"
and the "spiritual eating and drinking" of the bread and wine
"consecrated when they be separated to that holy use by Christ's
own words", viz., "that they maye be unto us the bodye and bloud
of thy moste derely beloved sonne Iesus Christe"—to quote the
words which stand immediately before the Institution-Narrative in
the Canon of Cranmer's 1549 rite, as in the Sarum Missal. It is,
therefore, misleading when Ratcliff concludes that except in the
process of eating and drinking the bread and wine of the Communion
are no more sacrament, for Cranmer, than the water in the baptismal
font.[30] The *Defence*, the *Answer*, and the 1549 rite consistently
distinguish between consecration and reception, "the whole ministration *and* reception", the "sacramental conversion" and the
"spiritual eating and drinking". How far Cranmer was responsible,
rather than Hooper and the Council, for the 1552 Prayer Book with
its wrecking of the structure of nearly every service in the 1549
Book and its much more Protestant doctrine, may, perhaps, never
be known. Professor Ratcliff has demonstrated that Cranmer and his
Anglican successors abandoned the medieval notion of a "moment
of consecration": he failed, however, to draw the obvious conclusion that for Cranmer, as for Luther, the sacramental presence of
Christ's body and blood lasted only from the recital of the words of
Institution until the last communicant had received the bread and
wine. During this time they were set apart for a "holy use"; there-
after they were no different from other bread and wine. Therefore,
no reservation of the sacrament was permitted either in the
Lutheran Church or in the Church of England.

28 Ibid., ii. p. 328.
29 *Works*, ed. Parker Society i. p. 174.
30 Art. cit., p. 234.

Cranmer and the English Reformers also shared with Luther (and with Calvin) the conviction that in the communion there is a "real partaking of the body and blood of Christ". Whilst Luther thought of the *ubiquitas carnis Christi*, and Calvin thought rather of Christ's glorified body localized in heaven, both stressed the importance of the union of the believer with the continually present Saviour which is achieved by obeying the command to "Take and eat". Calvin spoke not only for himself and those who thought as he did when he declared: "We all confess then with one mouth that in receiving the sacrament in faith, according to the ordinance of the Lord, we are truly made partakers of the real substance of the body and blood of Jesus Christ. How this is done, some may deduce better and explain more clearly than others."[31]

The present writer has attempted elsewhere[32] to show how Christian thinkers from the patristic period to the sixteenth century tried to "deduce better and explain more clearly than others" before them the deep mystery of the eucharistic presence of our Lord and its effects upon the worthy communicant. In so doing it was suggested that some used more realist and others more symbolist language. Indeed, the phrase "realist-symbolist" was coined to describe the doctrine of the latter, and, perhaps the phrase "symbolist-realist" ought to have been used of the doctrine of the former. Several reviewers have taken the author to task for making too hard and fast a distinction between the Augustinian and Ambrosian traditions.[33] This is a perfectly valid criticism. In an attempt to make crystal clear the basic difference between the two traditions, which became much clearer in the course of the eucharistic controversies of the ninth and eleventh centuries, and again in the sixteenth

---

[31] *Short Treatise*, in Reid, op. cit., p. 166.

[32] Dugmore, op. cit.

[33] E.g. by John N. Wright in *Month*, August 1959, pp. 110-13 and, with much more charity and considerably greater learning, by J.-D. Benoît in *Revue d'histoire et de philosophie religieuses* (1963), pp. 347-50. If Benoît tends to overstress the "realist" element in Augustine in reply to the author's description of his doctrine as "realist-symbolist", that element is undoubtedly present and Benoît rightly draws attention to the two uses of the phrase *virtus sacramenti* in Augustine: 1. the effect produced by the sacrament in the soul of the faithful recipient; 2. *"Je ne sais quoi de mystérieux qui rend le signe visible et matériel capable de produire cet effet spirituel"*—the *res saramenti* in Augustine's words, the "sacramental presence" (as distinguished from the "spiritual presence" in the faithful recipient) in Cranmer's words.

century, than it had ever been in the patristic period, the writer concedes that he may have presented the two views as more sharply defined and more mutually antagonistic than in fact they were in the age of the Fathers. There is, of course, much symbolist or figurative language to be found in Ambrose and much realist language in Augustine.[34] Even Paschasius Radbertus, who introduced the notion that at every Eucharist there is a new creation of the body of Christ (*in verbo et virtute Spiritus sancti nova fit creatura in corpore Creatoris*), later spoke of the flesh and blood of Christ as truly present on the altar, "but in a mystery, in figure". On the other hand, his opponent Ratramnus (who was instrumental in converting Ridley and then Cranmer from belief in transubstantiation and the propitiatory sacrifice of the Mass), whilst rejecting the notion that Christ's body and blood are present in the Eucharist *in veritate*, since this leaves no room for faith and removes the mystery of the sacrament, and holding that the change is made *spiritualiter* and not *corporaliter*, nevertheless localized the spiritual body of Christ *sub velamento*, under the veil of the material bread. That there were these two different understandings of the meaning of the real presence, the one stressing the actual conversion of the bread and wine by metabolism into the historical body and blood of Christ and the other stressing the symbolic and figurative sense of the Dominical Words of Institution, can scarcely be denied.

Despite Dr T. M. Parker's reminder that the whole meaning of symbolism to a Platonist was that the whole universe is sacramental, "the material being but the reflection of realities only to be grasped by the intellect, yet supremely objective"—the philosophical background, in the main, of all the early Fathers—and his contention that Augustine does not "ever seem conscious of any tension between his doctrine of *sacramentum* and *res* and what Ambrose had taught",[35] it remains true, as Dr Kelly has observed, that "there

---

[34] Ambrose and Augustine were not expressing mutually exclusive doctrines, nor were Stephen Gardiner and Cranmer; but their emphases were different. Even J. N. Wright is prepared to grant "that Christian eucharistic thought has always presented a two-fold aspect—realist and symbolist" (op. cit., p. 113).

[35] *JTS.*, n.s. xii (1961), p. 141

is no suggestion in his [Augustine's] writings of the conversion theory sponsored by Gregory of Nyssa and Ambrose. . . . His thought moves, as we should expect, much more along the lines laid down by Tertullian and Cyprian. . . . The body and blood are veritably received by the communicant, but are received sacramentally, or, as one might express it, *in figura*".[36] Batiffol had earlier noted the distinction which Augustine made between that which is seen and that which is believed, between the sign and the *res* (the invisible gift) of which the sign is the vehicle.[37] Dr Mascall is probably correct in suspecting (no more!) that these two views of the Eucharist "represented two elements in a whole rich complex of Eucharistic thought and that neither can be abandoned without impoverishment".[38] One feels that it is a little unfair of him, however, after quoting the writer's statement that "Catholicism, in the pre-scholastic period, was able to embrace both traditions", to comment that "what he [Dugmore] fails to see is that they can be no less fully embraced, and more profoundly reconciled, when their development is carried beyond the stage reached by the Lateran Council and the Later Middle Ages".[39] True, but the writer was not concerned with the theological situation of today: he was concerned with the sixteenth-century Reformation and its background in the Early Church and the Middle Ages. It might very cogently be argued that the Middle Ages in England lasted until *c*. 1560.

The post-Tridentine Roman tradition, the Lutheran, Reformed, and Anglican traditions all stem from the sixteenth-century Reformation and Counter-Reformation. They have been inherited by the twentieth-century, which has witnessed the birth of the Ecumenical Movement among the non-Roman Churches and the new spirit of theological inquiry and the desire for Christian fellowship expressed in Vatican Council II. One lesson which can, perhaps, be learnt from the theological controversies of the sixteenth century,

---

36 J. N. D. Kelly, *Early Christian Doctrines*, London, 1958, 448-9.

37 P. Batiffol, *Etudes d'histoire et de théologie positive*, 2me serie: *L'Eucharistie, la présence réelle et la transubstantiation*, Paris, 1905, p. 252. I refer here, as in *The Mass and the English Reformers*, to the first edition of this remarkable book, which was placed on the Index in 1911, and not to the much revised edition of 1913, to which Dr Parker refers (in its tenth edn, 1930).

38 *Corpus Christi*, 2nd edn, p. 186.

39 Ibid., pp. 187-8.

as from the Christological debates of the fourth and fifth centuries, is that sincere Christians of opposing parties, whether Nicene or Arian, Catholic or Protestant, were all concerned with the search for truth. Men were not prepared to suffer death under the Roman Emperors or the spiritual and secular powers in sixteenth-century Europe except for convictions deeply held which, they believed, affected their eternal destiny. The doctrines of the eucharistic sacrifice and the presence of Christ in the Eucharist were, thus, not merely matters of academic debate for the men and women of the Reformation Era. But beneath all the argument, the propaganda, the pamphleteering, most of them, if we except the radical sacramentarians and the anabaptists, were closer in their thinking than they realized at the time. They were all concerned, according to their own lights, and their traditionalist, scholastic, or humanistic backgrounds, to express the fulness of the Eucharist in the life and worship of the Church. If, when they disputed about the eucharistic presence of Christ, they sometimes seemed to be poles apart, in the last resort they were all concerned to make the anamnesis which the Lord enjoined at the Last Supper, to enter into ever deeper fellowship with him and with one another, and so to offer a sacrifice of praise and thanksgiving and of the Church united with Christ its Head, and to feed spiritually upon his body and blood by faith. This may have fallen short of the Catholic teaching of the medieval Church in the eyes of Eck or Cajetan. Unfortunately they did not see that Luther or Calvin were as sincere and devout as themselves and were concerned with the same eternal verities. Similarly, in England Gardiner and Cranmer both rejected a carnal interpretation of the real presence: in many ways they differed in their theology, but they both believed in a real partaking of the spiritual body and blood of Christ—even though they may have thought that they meant something rather different by "the spiritual body". "Now we see through a glass darkly, but then face to face." It was left to the Elizabethan, Richard Hooker, to remind men that, in face of the infinite mystery of the nature of God and of his dealings with men, human reason can only carry us so far. Beyond argument and theological speculation is the divine activity of love, which embraces all his children and imparts to the believer eternal life. "What moveth us," he says, "to argue of the manner how life should come by bread, our duty being here but to take what is offered?"[40] No one could accuse Richard Hooker of intellectual bankruptcy, but perhaps in this matter he chose the better path.

© C. W. Dugmore, 1968.

---

[40] Hooker, *Of the Laws of Ecclesiastical Polity*, V, lxvii.; 12 ed. Keble-Paget, Oxford, 1888, ii, p. 360.

5

THE EUCHARIST IN THE THEOLOGY OF THE NINETEENTH CENTURY

ALF HÄRDELIN

The Eucharist during the nineteenth century was not the *sacramentum unitatis*, but rather a point of division, separating not only church from church, but also different groups within the same church from one another. In the Church of England Anglo-Catholics and "Ritualists" were sharply divided from other groups of churchmen on the issue of the sacraments in general and of the Eucharist in particular. This antagonism was not altogether unique to England, for there are parallels to be found in protestant Churches on the Continent and in Scandinavia as well.

However, this complicated situation can only be understood, if we make clear as far as possible the legacy which the former centuries had handed over to the nineteenth. Thus it will be evident, that the problems concerning eucharistic faith and practice were not isolated problems, but rather they reflected a deep-seated conflict in Western intellectual and religious life as a whole. This conflict can be formulated as one threatening that *unity* which, according to traditional Christian theology, existed between God and creation, spirit and matter, historical past and historical present, individual and community. These unities, or rather syntheses, had in rationalist thought been broken asunder. What this meant to theology generally, and to the Eucharist in particular, is obvious.

Philosophical empiricism, culminating in Kantian epistemological criticism, made the doctrine of the real presence nonsensical, if not superstitious. If man's faculty of knowledge cannot penetrate into the supernatural world, or grasp the *Ding an Sich*, it is meaningless to speak about the presence of an unperceivable, spiritual substance given in, or with, material elements. Religion becomes reduced to morality, duty, or virtue, and the primary task of the Church and its ordinances is to strengthen men to fulfil the demands of the categorical imperative.

In Germany, where philosophy as a rule has had more direct influence on theology than in England, this moralistic concept of religion deeply influenced a number of theologians, even Catholic theologians. Among the latter there was perhaps no open denial of the Catholic dogma concerning the Eucharist, but rather a failure to make it meaningful otherwise than as an impetus to morality. Thus dogma and supernatural grace were tacitly put aside. There is no doubt but that this enlightened spirit more or less characterized many of those plans for liturgical and pastoral reform advocated in Germany around 1800 by such men as B. Werkmeister, V. A. Winter, and Ignaz von Wessenberg, the vicar-general of the diocese of Constance. According to Winter, external worship serves the purpose of improving men's notions about morality and of fostering willingness to perform its duties. In this system there is no place for a *cultus Dei* properly so called.[1] Worship is no longer an act whereby the world is dedicated to God and nature consecrated and glorified.

In England the deistic and rationalist tradition was carried on in a modified form during the former part of the century by the liberal theologians, of whom the most notable were the so-called Noetics: Thomas Arnold, R. D. Hampden, and Richard Whately.[2] As there are, according to them, no mysteries or mysterious doctrines in the Christian religion, so no mysterious virtues are, or can be, given through the sacraments. This rejection of sacramentally mediated grace was in accordance with Hoadly's deistic development of Zwingli's "memorialist" doctrine. It ought to be observed however that it was supported by a genuinely rationalistic argument, namely that the finite is incapable of communicating the infinite. To believe in "the mystical virtue of the sacraments" is to hold to nothing but "Judaizing superstitions", for "reason resting on faith" assures us,

1 See further A. Vierbach, *Die liturgischen Anschauungen des V. A. Winter*, Munich, 1929.
2 See further Y. Brilioth, *The Anglican Revival*, London 1925, chapter VI.

says Arnold, "of the utter incapability of any outward bodily action to produce in us an inward spiritual effect".[3]

However, when spirit and matter, or the external and the internal in the Church, are thus divorced from each other, religion might end either in naturalism or in a non-institutional and non-sacramental religion of the spirit. This latter tendency is clearly discernible in those Evangelical revivalist movements which arose in Germany as well as in England, partly as a protest against the prevailing rationalism. Here surely supernatural grace was not denied, but it was thought to be communicated to men independently of the "external" Church and its sacramental ordinances. These were perhaps not abandoned, but they tended to degrade to mere symbols and stimuli for the arising of feelings. The real Church was the invisible Church of the true believers.

The Romantic movement in Germany, supported by, and to a certain extent indistinguishable from, the idealistic philosophy of Schelling, F. Schlegel, and others, was, as Horst Fuhrmans says, permeated by one great passion : to overcome all dualisms, and to re-establish those syntheses which rationalism had disrupted.[4] God was for these thinkers not the God of the Deists, who once created the world and then left it to function according to its own inherent laws, like a mechanism. He was the living God, revealing himself in and through his creation, the Infinite manifesting himself in the finite. To the Romantic also, man stands in the centre, but not the independent man of the Enlightenment, living in accordance with his own autonomous reason. As being the crown of creation, man is rather a microcosm reflecting the macrocosm, the universe. Thus mankind is not a bundle of individuals, but an organism made up of its members.

These and other Romantic ideas were soon taken up by theologians, Catholic as well as Protestant, and applied by them to theology. In Landshut, Munich, and Lucerne, Catholic thinkers (P. B. Zimmer, F. von Baader, A. Gügler) interpreted the faith in Romantic categories.[5] In a modified form this was carried on by J. S. Drey and J. A. Möhler and their pupils in Tübingen. Among

---

[3] *Fragment on the Church*, 2nd edn, London, 1845, pp. 57, 61f, and 83.
[4] *Schellings Philosophie der Weltalter*, Düsseldorf, 1954, p. 252.
[5] A. Härdelin, "Kirche und Kult in der Luzerner theologischen Romantik", *Zeitschrift für katholische Theologie* 89 (1967), pp. 139-75.

Lutherans we find Romantic ideas to a greater or less extent also in the confessional Lutheranism of Kliefoth, and Kahnis and in the *Vermittlungstheologie* of I. A. Dorner. However, it is clearly impossible to deal here with the individual contributions of all these men to ecclesiology and eucharistic theology. We must limit ourselves to a sketch of some important and characteristic traits.

As the creation is a living manifestation of its Creator, so the Church is no mere external organization of men, founded on a *contrat social*, but the living expression, or the "body", of the Spirit animating that body. As art is essentially expression, so the Church and its ordinances of worship are like a work of art, revealing the Mind of the Spirit in created forms. One of the most famous books on the liturgy produced in Germany during the former part of the century is F. A. Staudenmaier's *Der Geist des Christenthums dargestellt in den heiligen Zeiten, in den heiligen Handlungen, und in den heiligen Kunst* (1835). The author decided, as he says in the preface, to expound the "Spirit of Christianity" through the holy ordinances, forms, and arts precisely because it is the Spirit who has manifested and revealed himself in and through them; they are his work. The forms of worship which have taken shape and developed through the centuries are not to be considered as the works of men's arbitrary will, but as developments from within of the Spirit.

Thus Romanticism awakened a new rejoicing in the concrete, in the bodily, and—to the theologians—in the visible Church and its sacraments. This was a gift of Romanticism to generations of divines. One of the leading Lutheran theologians, K. F. A. Kahnis, confessed with many others: "Nobody can belong to the invisible Church, who does not belong to the visible. The invisible Church is an abstraction." The sacraments to him are more than signs of the Word, for they stamp everybody to whom they are administered with an indelible character. They are bearers of the spirit and body of Christ, that is, of Christ himself in the fulness of his incarnate Person. The Calvinist doctrine of the sacraments is marked by that "rationalistic spirit which separates sign and content in the Supper, separates water and Spirit, word and Spirit, divine and human in Christ".[6]

The microcosm-macrocosm idea, to which allusion was made

---

6 *Die Lehre vom Abendmahle*, Leipzig, 1851, pp. 276f, and 424.

above, played a great rôle in the thought of some of our theologians. It is indeed not too much to say that this idea helped them to rediscover aspects of classical Christology which theology had formerly tended to obscure and, consequently, to rediscover the idea of the Church as a living organism. For if man is a microcosm of the universe, so is Christ not a mere individual, but the *makroanthropos*, the universal Man, summing up all men in his Person and so uniting them with the Father. Through the Incarnation the world was reconciled to God. This reconciliation, however, remains in the bosom of the Church as a perpetual mystery. The liturgy, and in particular the Eucharist, is nothing less than the continual manifestation and setting forth of this mystery, whereby mankind is restored to its original unity with God.

The communion which Christians have with each others is established by incorporation into the body of Christ, the universal Man. This is a supra-temporal communion, for it is rooted in that redemption which was no mere passing event in history, but which inaugurated the fulness of time. The objective redemption wrought on the cross remains in the Church; or rather, the Redeemer is there ever present, as F. A. Staudenmaier said, in order that the objective act might individualize itself, and so realize itself. This is a process, whereby Christ becomes ever more manifest in his body.[7]

Thus also the eucharistic sacrifice received a new meaning for the Catholic Romantics. As redemption was wrought by him who represents and sums up the whole of mankind, so the Eucharist is not merely the offering of Christ and the application of his merits. Christ cannot be divorced from his members, and thus the proper eucharistic victim is that humanity which has been assumed by Christ and which is his Church. The sacrifice is not only *for* the Church, but *of* the Church. Thus these Romantics of the early nineteenth century had already regained an "ecclesial" conception of the eucharist. We find it in the works of the Lucerne Romantics and it is further developed and modified by representatives of the Tübingen school.

In the Church of England it was the Oxford Movement which first articulated the protest against what was considered the rationalism of the age. Tractarian theology is surely far less dependent

---

[7] *Enzyklopädie der theologischen Wissenschaften*, Bd 1, 2. umgearb., sehr vermehrte Aufl., Mainz, 1840, p. 756.

on certain philosophic conceptions than was the German theology of which we have so far been writing. It had, however, the same passion for unity: unity *in* the Church between internal and external, and unity *of* the Church in time and space.[8]

Basic to the ecclesiology and sacramental doctrine of Newman and the other Tractarians is what they called the sacramental principle, the principle, that is, that God performs his saving work through the mediation or the instrumentality of created means which he has appointed. The Church itself is no mere external institution, but a means of grace. It is not only a means of grace to which the individual is referred, for grace is by its very nature social or "ecclesial".

> It has been [Newman says in an unpublished sermon of 1829] the great design of Christ to connect all his followers into one, and to secure this, he has lodged his blessing in the body collectively to oblige them to meet *together* if they would gain grace each for himself. The body is the first thing and each member in particular the second. The body is not made up of individual Christians, but each Christian has been made such in his turn by being *taken into the body*.

The Church is thus a living body, and its sacramental ordinances are no mere forms and shadows, but effectual signs of grace. In Christ's Kingdom time and space are annulled, for "the hour of his [Christ's] cross and passion [is] ever mystically present, though it be passed these eighteen hundred years. Time and space have no portion in the spiritual Kingdom which he has founded; and the rites of his Church are as mysterious spells by which he annuls them both".[9] What is here said about the Church in general, the Tractarians also applied to its liturgical forms. Exactly as did the German Romantics, these English divines came to regard the "external" Church, including its liturgical forms, as the outward expression of its inward, spiritual principle.

> The whole system of the Church [Newman says in a sermon of 1839], its discipline, and ritual, are all in their origin the spon-

---

[8] For a full study of Tractarian ecclesiology and eucharistic faith and practice, I might be allowed to refer to my work, *The Tractarian Understanding of the Eucharist*, Uppsala, 1965.

[9] J. H. Newman, *Parochial and Plain Sermons*, Standard edn, Vol. III, p. 277.

taneous and exuberant fruit of the real principle of spiritual religion in the hearts of its members. The invisible Church has developed itself into the Church visible, and its outward rites and forms are nourished and animated by the living power which dwells within. Thus every part of it is real, down to the minutest details.[10]

The church buildings with their ornaments are no mere works of art, but fruits of grace. The liturgical forms are no *adiaphora*, but, as indicating divine truths and conveying invisible privileges, they are in their nature sacramental.

This sacramental principle was of course of the greatest importance to Tractarian eucharistic theology in particular, for it led inevitably to the insight that the sacramental elements are not merely outward, empty symbols signifying the grace given, but that there is a real presence of Christ "under the form of bread and wine". This was to the Tractarians a mystery which faith alone could grasp. To try to explain it, was to intrude into secrets which God had given to men to exercise their faith upon. Christ's words "This is my body" cannot therefore be interpeted as metaphor, for, as R. Hurrell Froude said, with these words Christ "stated that which was more near the literal truth than could be expressed in any other language whatsoever". To explain them metaphorically was therefore to evacuate them of their meaning, or rather, to make them human.[11]

The eucharistic sacrifice presented another aspect of the problem of unity: the unity of Christ's sacrifice *then*, and the Church's sacrifice *now*. If subjective memory alone can bridge the gulf between then and now, the only acceptable doctrine of the eucharistic sacrifice would be to say: the Eucharist is an act whereby the Church recalls the goodness of Christ in giving his life for men. To teach a real sacrifice would then be to teach a new sacrifice, distinct in essence from Christ's.

Now, as Newman said, "Unity is [the] characteristic sacrament" of the New Covenant. Its priests are not priests at the side of, or independently of, the one High Priest, but as being his representatives, they share in the one priesthood of Christ. Similarly the

---

[10] Op. cit., Vol. V, p. 41.
[11] *Remains*, Vol: II, I, London, 1839, pp. 144ff.

eucharistic sacrifice is not essentially a new sacrifice, but a continuation, "a mysterious representation of his meritorious sacrifice in the sight of Almighty God". "As being instinct with that which they commemorate, they [the eucharistic celebrations] are absorbed and vivified in it."[12] If the Church is the mediatorial Kingdom, the Eucharist is the means he has given, not only to impart himself to his people, but to gather up the united worship of that mystical body which is humanity incorporated into Christ to be dedicated to the Father.

All this the Tractarians worked out in opposition to what they considered to be the rationalism of the Liberals and the emotional spiritualism of the Evangelicals. The "corner-stone and characteristic" of the church system is, as Pusey expressed it in an unpublished lecture of 1836, "God manifest in the flesh". The Church with all its sacramental ordinances has an incarnational structure. It is a mystery in earthly vessels, but at the same time a mystery transcending space and time.

Though the Oxford Movement then from one point of view was a reaction, the Movement was not intellectually reactionary. For if we study it against its European background, it becomes evident that Tractarian theology was, at least in its first creative stage, no mere restoration of the thinking of ages gone by. On the contrary, it showed itself to be a fresh expression of old doctrines in the idiom and with the categories of a universal European movement of culture and thought. Tractarianism was essentially dynamic, and not static; synthetic, and not one-sided.

It is nevertheless equally obvious that neither the Continental theology we have studied, nor the Tractarians in England won the battle in their day. Tractarian sacramental theology became the spiritual food of generations of Anglicans in the Anglo-Catholic Movement, who developed what the pioneers had begun. It substantiated a far-reaching revival of liturgical worship, it nourished an intense desire for the reunion of Christendom, it inspired many men and women to heroic pastoral and missionary work at home and abroad, but—it remained the belief of a party. When thus for

---

12 *Lectures on the Doctrine of Justification*, Standard edn, pp. 198f., and 205; *Lectures on the Scripture Proof of the Doctrines of the Church*, (Tracts for the Times 85), 3rd edn, London, 1842, p. 40.

instance William Goode in 1856 published his work, *The Nature of Christ's Presence in the Eucharist*, it was aimed at opposing the "Fictitious Real Presence" taught by Denison, R. I. Wilberforce, and Pusey. To this Evangelical writer the Eucharist is "altogether a *spiritual* transaction, one in which our spirits only can take part".[13] There neither is, nor can there be, a presence of Christ's body and blood in any way connected with the earthly elements, for earthly things cannot really be instrumental in a spiritual transaction. It was on this philosophical principle, and not only on the question whether Tractarian doctrine was compatible with Anglican formularies or not, that Goode and many before and after him turned against Tractarian sacramentalism.

Whatever theological differences there might have been between Goode and his fellow-Evangelicals and the Liberals of Oriel, and the writers who in 1860 produced *Essays and Reviews*, they were unanimous in their rejection of the sacramental principle. The key-word of the theology of *Essays and Reviews* is *progress*; progress was the key-word of the time, in science, in history-writing, and in philosophy. The "Education of the World" of which F. Temple wrote was one by which the world was brought successively from childhood to maturity, from the law to the Spirit teaching within, from the letter to the spirit. The fruit of spiritual progress is toleration, whose tendency it is "to modify the early dogmatism by substituting the spirit for the letter, and practical religion for precise definitions of truth". The same "progress" is to be found in the development of men's worship of God. While under the Law, it "consisted almost entirely of sacrifices". The Jewish people in the captivity, that is, far away from temple and sacrifices, "first learned that the spiritual part of worship could be separated from the ceremonial, and that of the two the spiritual was far the higher". "Progress" thus means the disconnection of spirit and matter, and not their unification in a higher synthesis. The Incarnation is in that respect a passing event in the history of mankind. It is not the enduring principle of the Church, for "first comes the Law, then the Son of Man, then the Gift of the Spirit".[14] Conceptions of a "virtual presence of the Lord Jesus everywhere that he is preached, re-

[13] Op. cit., Vol. I, London, 1856, p. 89.
[14] *Essays and Reviews*, London, 1860, pp. 43, 10, and 5.

membered, and represented, and of the continual force of His spirit in His words" are, as another contributor to the *Essays* maintained, "truer" than those of a "corporeal" presence.[15]

In this way liberal English divines attempted to reconcile the Christian faith with what contemporary science and philosophy seemed to them to require. Their intention thereby was no doubt a constructive one: by thus "purifying" the "spiritual" religion from the "gross" conceptions in which more "primitive" ages had dressed it, they were, so they thought, faithful to the Mind of the Spirit. On the Continent, however, biblical criticism took a far more radical shape. While the older rationalism had rescued the letter at least of the Bible by moralistic and utilitarian interpretations of the texts, a new school under the leadership of D. F. Strauss in Germany and E. Renan in France declared everything "supernatural" to be Oriental myth without historical or rational foundations. Strauss wrote towards the end of his life that "As baptism . . . has lost its real meaning, thus also has it fared with the Lord's supper in regard to the atonement, nothing remaining now but the repulsive Oriental metaphor of drinking the blood and eating of the body of a man".[16]

To many Churchmen, Anglican and Lutheran as well as Roman Catholic, it had become obvious that there was no salvation to be found for the Church by compromises with the "world", or through dialogues with the *Zeitphilosophie*. In England, old-fashioned Tractarians like H. P. Liddon uncompromisingly clung to the old ideas of biblical inspiration. In France, revolutionary ideas had at an early stage been opposed by a theological traditionalism, which rested on a complete distrust of reason. In Germany, where Thomism had never been quite extinct, the Jesuit J. Kleutgen became the initiator of Neo-Thomism through his works *Theologie der Vorzeit* (3 vols. 1853-70) and *Philosophie der Vorzeit* (2 vols. 1860-63). The prevailing theological confusion and the rapid unsettlement of the faith brought about by the *Zeitgeist* could only be remedied, so it was thought, through a return to the safe principles of St Thomas

---

15 H. B. Wilson, op. cit., pp. 203f.
16 *Der alte und der neue Glaube*, E. T. *The Old Faith and the New*, by Mathilde Blind, London, 1874, p. 105.

and his school. There the solid weapons were to be found whereby liberal and revolutionary attacks could be defeated.[17]

With this return to Thomism there also came a greater precision and "correctness" in eucharistic theology. The gain however also meant a loss: the corporate and cosmic-eschatological aspects of the Eucharist, which were beginning to be rediscovered in so many works of the former part of the century, had no chance to come to maturity. The seed was sown, but it never had time to flower and to affect the liturgical worship of the Church. The Eucharist became, perhaps even more strongly than during the Baroque age, essentially the adorable Presence of our Lord. The sacrifice was thought of predominantly as the sacrifice of Christ, whose saving fruits were dispensed at Holy Communion, but not so much as the sacrificial action of the whole Church, head and members. The unity between sacrament and sacrifice did not altogether vanish from the sight of the theologians, but it did not find liturgical expression. High Mass without Communion and Low Mass with Communion, or even Communion outside the Mass, was the typical arrangement in Roman Catholic as well as in Anglo-Catholic churches.

It was left to this century to take up the thread from the earlier part of the former century, though many of those who expound and practise these and similar ideas today are ignorant of having had any forerunners in the nineteenth century. It is thus common among writers on the Liturgical Movement to regard the liturgical endeavours of the former century as sheer "antiquarian reconstruction". This is Father Bouyer's characterization of the nineteenth century. As we can see from what has been said above, this is not the whole truth. What Father Bouyer has mainly in view is that French movement which, as far as the liturgy is concerned, was inaugurated by Dom Guéranger, the founder of Solesmes, and the author of very influential works on liturgical questions. The greatest weakness of his enterprise was, Father Bouyer says, "that it could not have become the real worship of any actual congregation of its own period. It could become only the worship of that artificial

---

[17] For a masterly survey of the development of German Catholic theology, see B. Welte, "Zum Strukturwandel der katholischen Theologie im 19. Jahrhundert, *Auf der Spur des Ewigen*, Freiburg, 1965, pp. 380-409.

monastic congregation which Dom Guéranger had brought into existence simply in order to carry it out".[18]

There is no doubt but that Guéranger supported his ideas with many arguments which later liturgical research has proved to be historically unsound. His intentions however are not sufficiently described, if we label them as a manifestation of mere antiquarianism. He transferred Ultramontane ideas of Church unity and authority to the liturgical field, and worked for the entire expulsion of the Gallican rites, since Church unity, so he argued, required liturgical uniformity.[19]

Similar ideas also found their way into Tractarian circles in England. The far-reaching consequences of this should not be overlooked. The unity of the Church of England had already been severely threatened through the direction which Tractarian theology had taken. This theology was based on a view of doctrinal authority which brought about new loyalties, but therefore also increased tensions. The essential ecclesiastical boundary had to be drawn, according to the Oxford divines, not between the Church of England itself and other Churches, but between two "systems", the Catholic and the Protestant. There was a "Catholic" Church which was not altogether identical with any one denomination. Now the Tractarians came to accept, and their followers more and more to put into practice, a theory of liturgical uniformity which led to a thorough romanizing of the forms of Anglo-Catholic worship. This of course meant an additional and more serious, because far more conspicuous, cause of tension between the different parties within the Church of England. The steady romanizing of Anglo-Catholic worship at that time was not, as has so often been maintained, due simply to liturgical ignorance or to a childish, and therefore irresponsible, desire for imitation. It must be understood as the expression of a conscious desire visibly to manifest unity in the Catholic faith. Thus later generations only drew the extremest consequences of what Newman had said already in 1842 : "if we claim to *be* the Church, let us act *like* the Church, and we shall *become* the Church."[20]

---

[18] *Life and Liturgy*, London, 1965, p. 12; American edn, with title, *Liturgical Piety*, Notre Dame, Ind., 1955, p. 12.

[19] See further O. Rousseau, o.s.b., *Histoire du mouvement liturgique*, Paris, 1945, esp. pp. 21-4.

[20] *Sermons Bearing on Subjects of the Day*, Standard edn, p. 391.

However, there were also at the end of the century theologians and churchmen who regarded themselves as orthodox, but who nevertheless thought that a dialogue between the Church and the "world" was still necessary and possible. This dialogue then would not mean the surrender of the Christian faith to the *Zeitgeist*, but a dialectic encounter and confrontation to the benefit of all involved, and to the benefit of the future. The Kingdom of God was to these theologians a dynamic principle of unification. The Church must not become a ghetto, but show itself to be the means of consecration of all human endeavours, intellectual and artistic as well as social. The Bread of Life is the Bread for the world's life; the sacrament of unity is the means of unifying total humanity with God. True progress is not brought about by secularization, but by sanctification in the Incarnate, the God-Man.

These thoughts, laid down by several theologians and apologists on the Continent, were brilliantly expressed in England by the men who collaborated in the famous book of essays called *Lux Mundi*, which first appeared in 1889. In these "Studies in the Religion of the Incarnation", the Romantic and Tractarian sacramentalism meets us again, but recast in accordance with the changed intellectual and cultural atmosphere. The Incarnation thus has a cosmic significance; redemption is "a means to an end, and that end the reconsecration of the whole universe to God".[21] The Christian religion is necessarily sacramental, for "the spiritual forces with which he [Christ] would renew the face of the earth were to be exerted through material instruments". This sacramental principle is the most forceful "defence of the material against the insults of sham spiritualism", and, at the same time, it is a "perpetual prophecy of the glory that shall be revealed in us".[22] The sacraments, however, are also social, as they are the appointed means to build up and renew the human brotherhood. In the liturgy "the whole Church devotes itself for the good of the whole world". The Eucharist has thus become the centre of unity:

> in it each Christian has taken up his own life, his body and soul, and offered it as a holy, lively, and reasonable sacrifice unto God,

[21] J. R. Illingworth, in *Lux Mundi*, ed. by Charles Gore, 12th edn, London, 1891, p. 134.
[22] F. Paget, op. cit., pp. 307, 309, and 314.

a service in spirit and in truth: and deeper still, he recognizes that his life does not stand alone; through the common ties of humanity in Christ he is linked on by a strange solidarity with all mankind; his life depends on theirs and theirs on his, and so he offers it not for himself only but for all.

Consequently schism is a sin, for it "prevents the full work of brotherhood, of knitting Christian with Christian in common worship".[23]

The picture which we have attempted to draw of the Eucharist in the nineteenth century has shown us much strife and very many ways of interpretation. Neither those who tried to build up a eucharistic theology by a positive encounter with contemporary thought and culture, nor those who fled to the ways of the past succeeded in gaining general assent. However, under the surface of these strifes and confusions one can see the growth of a unifying factor, namely the revived grasp of the Church as a living organism, humanity incorporated into Christ. Thus the foundations were laid for that reorientation of eucharistic theology and worship which we witness today, and which has now become a means of approach between Christians. For if the Eucharist unites heaven and earth, and past and present in the kingdom of God, it cannot be thought of without awakening also an intense longing for the unity of all Christians, and the unity of all men in Christ.

---

23 W. Lock, op. cit., pp. 280 and 287.

6

LITURGY
IN THE TWENTIETH CENTURY

JOHN WILKINSON

As the twentieth century opened, the English domestic scene was outwardly calm. Social life was still sufficiently stratified for the clergy to see themselves as life members of a powerful and well-defined middle class. Although the calm did not extend to matters of ecclesiastical party politics, it could at least be said that they were no longer conducted by litigation.

The lawsuits were over, but they left behind them bitterness and disorder. When a Royal Commission presented its findings on ritual matters in 1906, it had little more positive to say than that the legislation affecting public worship in Britain was too narrow, and that the machinery of discipline had broken down. There was little hope of obedience or peace so long as the Prayer Book remained unchanged, and gradually the church authorities began to take tentative steps to provide a new one. But it was not until 1912 that the Archbishops took the step of appointing an Advisory Committee on Liturgical Questions, and even then its work was hampered by its narrow terms of reference, and delayed through the outbreak of the 1914-18 war.

These delays only served to attach the parties more firmly to their conception of the *status quo*. When the war ended, the Evangelicals were firmly wedded to sung Mattins as their main Sunday service, though it was followed by a celebration of the Holy Communion at least once a month. Anglo-Catholics were equally attached to a pattern of communicating Low Masses on a Sunday, which complemented sung Mass as the main service, though this was seldom an occasion when the people received Holy Communion.

Between these two extremes were churchmen who wished to be loyal to the 1662 Book, but refused to interpret it either in exclusive fidelity to the protestant aspects of the Reformation, or in an attempt to adapt it to Roman practice. Some sought an English tradition of ceremonial in the prayer books of Salisbury before the Reformation, which they adapted with more or less success to the requirements of the Book of Common Prayer and the developed forms of worship in Chichester Cathedral were among the most exact and definite examples of this "Sarum" group.

Evangelicals looked back, Anglo-Catholics looked at Rome, and the Sarum enthusiasts studied the late Middle Ages. But the scholars like W. H. Frere and F. E. Brightman, who were looking much further back to the primitive liturgies, did not publish their findings in a form which was popularly read, and party-consciousness was a far more vital force than scholarship. It was, moreover, within the context of party allegiances that liturgical obedience found its interpretation. Evangelicals saw their obedience to the Prayer Book and the law of the land as a bastion against the liberal and modernist movements around them as well as against the High Churchmen, and fought to bring those who differed from them into the same obedience. Their position was weakened by the Royal Commission. Anglo-Catholics saw their obedience as loyalty to a Catholic tradition wider and better founded than a national Prayer Book which was in fact a Reformation compromise. But in obeying many of the liturgical decrees of Rome, they were forced to be selective, and the number of decisions they had to make as individuals or as members of a party much weakened their understanding of a more normal obedience. Gradually they became accustomed to their non-conformity.

Among Roman Catholics the idea of obedience was far more straightforward. Apart from the continuance of some ancient pre-Reformation rites here and there in the West, and in the Eastern Churches united to Rome, there was one Roman liturgy and variations due to local custom were minor. No one doubted that the Eucharist was the main service to which the faithful must come, but in 1905 Pope Pius X had to remind them that they ought to make their Communion more frequently. His initiative gave rise to a further examination of the part which the people ought to play in the liturgy, and these studies gave birth to the Liturgical Movement, whose inspiration came specially from the Benedictine abbeys of Mont-César in Belgium and Maria Laach in Germany.

The Liturgical Movement became a revolution which has not only outgrown its modest origins but has also, in its essentials, been officially approved by the Second Vatican Council. At its roots lay the determination to restore a positive use of the ancient and admirable Roman rite, and to see the possibilities it afforded for truly corporate worship. The Liturgical Movement constituted a criticism not of the text of the rite—which was the Anglican problem—but of its use. By interpreting its meaning, and freeing it from its many obscurities, the protagonists of the Liturgical Movement sought to make it once again a rite which was shared by all present, according to their different capacities.

To many Roman Catholics, and also to the English Anglo-Catholics who used Roman books of devotion, the Mass was usually seen as the crown of private devotion. All the life of the individual, in work and prayer, found its expression in the prayers said as the eucharistic sacrifice was offered for him. The act of Communion itself was to some extent a private matter, and, except on a few great feasts, the people's Communion was not seen as an essential feature of the Mass. The Liturgical Movement, undeterred by the difficulty that the Mass was in Latin, set itself to demonstrate that the Mass was the crowning act of the Christian community. It is remarkable how much its leaders were able to achieve without disobedience.

These studies were only beginning on the Continent when the English revision saw the light. In 1927 the Church Assembly gave consideration to a new Prayer Book which represented not only the seven years of direct work which had been devoted to it by the Assembly's own Prayer Book Revision Committee, but also the results of earlier work which had begun soon after 1906.

So far as the eucharistic rite was concerned, the book met with some determined opposition. The proposed Prayer of Consecration included soon after the narrative of the Last Supper a paragraph saying, "Hear us, O merciful Father, we humbly beseech thee, and with thy Holy and Life-giving Spirit vouchsafe to bless and sanctify both us and these thy gifts of Bread and Wine, that they may be unto us the Body and Blood of thy Son". This epiclesis was unwelcome to many Evangelicals, who felt either that it was an unnecessary addition to the 1662 form of prayer to which they were accustomed, or that if it was felt to be necessary, it constituted an alteration in the doctrine of the Church of England.[1] In fact the 1549 Prayer Book had had a comparable form of words, which appeared before the account of the Last Supper, and the Books of 1552 and 1662 had omitted them. But the epiclesis was unwelcome also to the large majority of Anglo-Catholics, who found no such words in the Roman Canon, and believed that they undermined the usual western understanding of the Consecration, which was that the elements became the body and blood of Christ when the priest said Christ's words in the narrative of the Supper. W. H. Frere, then bishop of Truro, who had played a great part in the construction of the rite, believed that the epiclesis was desirable in itself. But although the historical arguments for its inclusion were extremely weighty, he felt that it should not be imposed on all. His views are expressed in a letter[2] written in February 1927, on the eve of the proposed book's final revision :

> I have never been a believer in getting all to rally to one Canon. If they are not to be allowed to have two of them, and I expect public opinion is too strong against that to be resisted, then I think the best way is to have a Canon like what is suggested in the new book, but to put as a second paragraph in the prayer a clause, "Hear us, O merciful Father" like the one in our present Prayer Book, and to treat this as the alternative to the other clause lower down, putting a footnote at the bottom of the prayer to say, "Only one of the clauses beginning 'Hear us, O merciful Father' is to be said". In that way both views would be satisfied; and I think there is a great deal to be said for doing it that way. I don't think any attempt to make us all agree in one will ever succeed. The differences are too ancient and too deep, and after all most people will be content to use either, provided they are both there.

Frere's suggestion about alternatives was rejected. There was

---

1 See R. C. D. Jasper, (ed.) *Walter Howard Frere, his Correspondence on Liturgical Revision and Construction*, Alcuin Club, S.P.C.K., 1954, p. 62. n. 2.
2 Ibid., p. 115.

still a desire to find one text which all could obey; and although the proposed text passed the Church Assembly by two-thirds majorities both in 1927 and 1928, it never became law, since it was rejected in Parliament.

Nor did the eventual production of the 1928 Book make much difference in practice. Though the bishops authorized its use, in defiance of Parliament, the only part of the eucharistic rite which gained any wide acceptance was its Prayer for the Church. England was faced with the same problems as before. The existing machinery for discipline was still further weakened by the bishops' refusal to obey Parliament; and at 11 a.m. on a Sunday the Anglo-Catholics continued to celebrate their sung Eucharist as usual, while the Evangelicals attended Mattins.

The English deadlock was not, however, the only aspect of the Anglican scene. Not only was there a small but increasing number of parishes which emphasized the importance of a solemn Sunday celebration to which the whole parish should come and receive Communion, but also in other parts of the world there were Anglicans who had produced, or were on the brink of producing, their own local rites for Holy Communion.

The local rites grew up in differing circumstances, but none in the context of bitter party strife which formed the background of revision in England. The first of them took shape in about 1910 in a fairly monochrome area with a strong bishop. It was the Swahili rite, which was compiled by Bishop Frank Weston for use in the diocese of Zanzibar, and was, to all intents and purposes, a return to the English pattern of 1549. Two of the others, those of the Episcopal Churches of the U.S.A. and Scotland, were conservative revisions in the tradition of the earlier Scottish rite of 1764. The new South African rite of the same year, 1929, was very close in spirit to the English rite of 1928, though it included in the Prayer of Consecration both the elements which Frere had suggested as alternatives in his letter of 1927. The kinship between the English and South African rites owed much to the fact that Frere acted as one of the principal advisers to the South African revision committee. The Bombay Liturgy (1923-33) was a conscious attempt to produce an eastern liturgy for an eastern part of the Church, and, though thoroughly scholarly, it was too elaborate to secure general approbation. In a slightly revised form it is still included in a supplement to the Prayer Book of the Church of India, Pakistan, Burma, and Ceylon.

Another liturgy of those days deserves special mention, not so much on account of its form, which was (again owing to Frere's advice) very like that of 1928, as for the desires which brought it into being. The Bishop of Northern Rhodesia (now Zambia) hoped to secure the use of a common liturgy in the three dioceses of Zanzibar, Nyasaland (now Malawi), and Northern Rhodesia, which owed their origins to the work of the Universities' Mission to Central Africa. Between 1922 and 1929 a rite took shape, but it did not succeed in ousting the Swahili rite in Zanzibar, and was used in a slightly different form in Nyasaland, which did not admit the use of its epiclesis. In this it differed from all the other new rites so far mentioned, except the Swahili.

All these rites sought to clarify the structure of the liturgy, and to restore as far as possible the primitive elements which were either omitted or obscured in the existing Prayer Books. The liturgies were designed for use in the vernacular, but in their English versions they usually retained strong reminiscences of the language originated by Cranmer, and often reproduced the actual prayers which he had written. They constituted a family of liturgies which, despite their variety were all clearly related to each other, with the single exception of the Bombay Liturgy, which looked almost exclusively to pre-Reformation eastern sources. This family was, moreover, quite distinct from the non-Anglican revisions taking shape at the same time, like the new *Book of Common Order*, which was published in 1928 by the United Free Church of Scotland, even though this explicitly set out to restore the use of traditional and primitive eucharistic material.

Though from a legal point of view the thirties were little different from the early years of the century, society had undergone a transformation. The 1914-1918 war had loosened the class-structure, and released many people from a purely local perspective. Respectability and religious scepticism could go side by side in a way which it had once been wise to conceal, and the conventional habit of churchgoing began to disappear. These developments made it urgent that parishes should see their services in a new light. In the event this light came from the Roman Liturgical Movement.

Parishes which had pioneered the Sunday Parish Communion had already gained valuable experience,[3] and by 1937 their practical knowledge, and the lessons of the Liturgical Movement on the Continent, had reached a stage which enabled Father Gabriel Hebert, s.s.m. to publish the collection of essays called *The Parish Communion.*

"By 'the Parish Communion'," wrote Father Hebert, "is meant the celebration of the Holy Eucharist, with the communion of the people, in a parish church, as the chief service of the day". This definition was a double-edged sword. Not only did it strike at those who still thought of Mattins as the main service. It was a criticism also of those who were accustomed to attending celebrations of the Eucharist at which the priest was the only communicant. Christ's sacrament was neither to be subordinated to Mattins, nor was it to be one of several celebrations on the same day. It was to be *"the* service—*the* divine Liturgy" for the which the entire parish community assembled, and the ideal was that there should be no supplementary celebrations.

With the publication of *The Parish Communion* many parishes began to look once again at their worship, and to adopt some of the new principles. But nearly all of them found that the ideal of having only one celebration a Sunday was more than they could achieve. In the end only a few parishes experienced the full teaching of Parish Communion about the parish as a worshipping community, and this was particularly unfortunate in a time when the place of the Church in society was changing. If the Parish Communion had spread thirty years earlier, congregations would have represented complete social units. At it was, they represented only those who still "belonged" and were willing to come to their parish church. But a great many parishes gained from the book. Many started an offertory procession—which the book encouraged on the grounds that the offering is "the offering of the people's labour, originally made in kind, as an acknowledgement of powers and gifts Godgiven";[4] and many found in the Parish Communion a way of renewal in worship which depended not on revised wording for the rite, but on a positive theological interpretation and use of the elements it already contained.

---

[3] See, "The Parish Communion After 25 Years" by H. de Candole, *The Parish Communion Today,* edited by D. M. Paton, S.P.C.K., 1962, pp. 1-5.

[4] Hebert, op. cit., p. 245.

In retrospect it is impossible to ignore the great pastoral benefits which the Parish Communion has brought to English church life. Over a large part of the Church of England it has succeeded in restoring the Eucharist to a position of prominence far greater than at the opening of the century. But the movement has not been without its dangers. Father Hebert himself foresaw some of them when he wrote "We ought indeed to encourage our people to make frequent Communion; but in doing so we must not allow them to think lightly of the privilege".[5] Some parishioners have found themselves unexpectedly making their Communion simply because they happened to be coming to church. Too often they seemed to be unaware of the responsibilities of this act. The offertory procession is not essential to the people's participation in the eucharist, and may even divert attention from the main sacrifice, which is not that of our work, but the sacrifice once offered in Christ's cross and resurrection.

Just at a time when pastoral considerations were beginning to replace legalistic or party views of the Eucharist came the Second World War. The Bishops made vain proposals between 1938 and 1942 for a new liturgical text, but they came to nothing. In 1945 however, a book was published which did much to prepare the ground for a reconsideration of the liturgy not only in its Cranmerian details, but in its basic structure. Dom Gregory Dix's *The Shape of the Liturgy* was, when it appeared, by far the most comprehensive, readable, and usable history of eucharistic development in the English language, and has been used with profit by members of every denomination. In many details Dix was wrong. His interpretation of the Last Supper has received little support, and few would agree with his arbitrary treatment of the text of Hippolytus. But none of these blemishes affected his main thesis that in its essential shape the Eucharist was a fourfold sequence of acts— Taking, Giving Thanks, Breaking, and Distribution. For many people this sequence provided a new key to their understanding of the service.

In 1948, just after the war, the Church of South India came into being. Many Anglicans were doubtful about the status of this united

5 Hebert, op. cit., p. 29.

Church, but in 1950 it produced a Liturgy which they welcomed with enthusiasm.

The committee which produced the C.S.I. Liturgy gloried in the fact that it was composed of non-experts. But it called on many experts for advice, and took full account of the work of Dom Gregory Dix. This liturgy was designed to allow the people as full a measure of vocal participation as possible. Learning the lessons of the Bombay Liturgy, it provided for congregational responses at many points in the service, including the Prayer of Consecration itself. Like the liturgies of Bombay and Ceylon (1933-38) it gave the Intercession in the form of a litany. And it provided for the reading of an Old Testament Lesson before the Epistle.

English Anglicans had feared that a Church formed by union with non-Anglicans would want a liturgy with its roots no deeper than the Reformation. They were amazed to find that the C.S.I. had produced a Eucharist with a more Catholic shape than anything of their own. Quite apart from its value as an example the new liturgy demonstrated that sound Catholic structure could no more be regarded as the monopoly of any particular party.

The C.S.I. Liturgy first appeared in 1950 only for "optional use on special occasions", and it was decided that it should be reconsidered after a number of years. This period of experimental use was valuable, and when the reconsideration took place in 1954, some slight revisions were made before the liturgy was authorized for general use. But though the liturgy has been authorized, it is not yet universally adopted, and many C.S.I. congregations still retain the rites which they used before the union.

No better compliment could have been paid the C.S.I. Liturgy than the recommendations made by the Lambeth Conference in 1958. It urged that "a chief aim of Prayer Book Revision should be to further that recovery of the worship of the Primitive Church which was the aim of the compilers of the first Prayer Books of the Church of England".[6] And among the suggestions "for the further recovery of . . . elements of the worship of the Primitive Church" made by the committee concerned with revision, the five which were relevant to the Eucharist were all in line with the text of the C.S.I. service.

---

[6] *The Lambeth Conference 1958*, S.P.C.K. and Seabury Press, 1958, Resolution 74 (c), p. 1. 47.

The same Lambeth Conference also requested that a committee should be set up "to prepare recommendations for the structure of the Holy Communion service which could be taken into consideration by any Church or Province revising its Eucharistic rite,"[7] since the Prayer Book Revision Committee had expressed the belief that "There are reasons for hoping that it is now possible to work towards a liturgy which will win its way throughout the Anglican Communion".[8] They explained that, far from counselling a "return to those rigid and legalistic ideas of uniformity which prevailed for some centuries", they were suggesting no more than a basic pattern, which would be sufficiently variable to meet local situations and needs. The Committee regretted that there should be alternative rites within a single province.

The Committee made no definite recommendation about the inclusion of an epiclesis in any future rites. What was particularly interesting about their report was the inclusion of two excellent notes on the eucharistic sacrifice and consecration, in both of which they acknowledged their indebtedness to a Roman Catholic scholar, Père Louis Bouyer. Liturgical revision was seen not merely as an Anglican exercise, but as a process involving a common Christian heritage of worship and of truth.

Unfortunately no less than four provinces already had their revisions at so advanced a stage by the time of the Conference that they were unable to incorporate its suggestions. It had recommended that the Offertory should be more closely connected with the Prayer of Consecration. But the new liturgies of 1959 (Canada, the West Indies, and Japan) and 1960 (India) all separated Offertory and Prayer of Consecration by an intercession, and only in the Indian liturgy was this intercession provided in the recommended litany form. It was also recommended that "the events for which thanksgiving is made in the Consecration Prayer are not to be confined to Calvary, but include thanksgiving for all the principal 'mighty works of God', especially the resurrection and the ascension of our Lord, and his return in glory".[9] All the new rites made mention of these mysteries in the anamnesis, but only the West Indies and Japan made any systematic attempt to do so in the first part of the

7 Ibid., Resolution 76, p. 1. 48.
8 Ibid., p. 2. 81.
9 Ibid., p. 2. 81.

Consecration Prayer. The Indian liturgy at this point included a mention of the incarnation as well as Calvary, but the Canadian rite remained content with the formula of 1662.

It was ironic that the only thoroughly Lambeth-like liturgy to appear in 1959 was not Anglican, but that of the Reformed Protestant community of Taizé. The Anglican response to the Lambeth recommendations took five years to produce.

The archbishops of the Anglican Communion in Africa agreed in the hope that a new liturgy might form a bond between Anglicans all over that Continent, which at the time used at least five different rites. One of these archbishops, the Most Reverend Leslie Brown, (now Bishop of St Edmundsbury and Ipswich), had been instrumental in the preparation of the C.S.I. liturgy, and had been secretary of the Lambeth Conference Revision Committee. He now became the architect of the new one. It took three years to prepare, and in the final form in which it appeared in 1964 was an example of all the virtues which Lambeth had required. It showed a strong family likeness with the Liturgy of C.S.I., but was much more clear and economical, and certainly ranks among the best rites ever produced in the Anglican Communion.

A point of particular interest in the new *Liturgy for Africa*[10] is its treatment of the problem of the epiclesis, which had caused such trouble in Britain in 1927 and 1928. Historically although nearly all ancient rites except the Roman contain an epiclesis, it is sometimes a prayer that God will consecrate the elements, and sometimes a prayer for the sanctification of those who will receive them. It seems probable that the form of the epiclesis was not fixed in the earliest stages of liturgical development, but that the eucharistic prayer as a whole had a trinitarian form in which God the Father was blessed at the opening of the prayer for his mighty works; it went on with blessing for the works done in Christ; and before the doxology there was some mention of Holy Spirit in Holy Church, rather in the style of the Creeds.[11] Here is the relevant section of the *Liturgy for Africa*:

[10] Published in this country by S.P.C.K., 1964. The other Anglican rites so far mentioned are collected, together with the C.S.I. rite, in B. Wigan, *The Liturgy in English*, O.U.P., London, 1962.

[11] For this theory see G. Every, *Basic Liturgy*, Faith Press, 1961, pp. 71-90.

Accept us in him [Christ], we beseech thee, and grant that all we who are partakers of this holy communion may be filled with thy Holy Spirit and made one in thy holy Church. . . .

The two latest Anglican rites for experimental use are those for Wales (1966) and England (1967), both of which exhibit a general pattern very like that of the *Liturgy for Africa*. It seems that a "basic pattern" of the kind desired by the 1958 Lambeth Conference is beginning to appear. If we use these three rites and that of Taizé as a basis we find it is roughly as follows:

I

1. A Preparation

A hymn or a psalm may be sung at the entry of the Ministers. Then may be said the Collect for Purity asking the aid of the Holy Spirit, and an act of penitence, including Confession and Absolution, though this is postponed to another position in the proposed English rite. *Gloria in Excelsis* may then be sung. This section ends with the Greeting, "Let us Pray", and Collect of the Day.

2. The Ministry of the Word

Three lessons may be read, interspersed with singing, and followed by the sermon. On certain days a Creed is said.

3. The Intercession

An intercessory litany is used, not necessarily led by the Celebrant. Some rites allow a short prayer as an alternative.

These three sections complete the first part of the rites. At this point various provisions are made for a prayer of preparation for Communion (Africa), an act of penitence (England), and for Banns and notices (England).

2

1. The Peace

The Anglican rites provide for the greeting "The Peace of the Lord be always with you" at this point, and the African rite suggests a gesture of fellowship to accompany the greeting. The Taizé liturgy postpones the Peace and Gesture until just before the Communion (a position corresponding with that in the Roman Mass).

2. *Bringing the gifts*

With or without public prayers, the gifts of the people and the bread and wine are taken to the sanctuary, and the bread and wine placed on the holy Table.

3. *The Thanksgiving*

After the usual dialogue the celebrant begins the Thanksgiving, or Prayer of Consecration, praising God for Creation, the sending of the Son, and the incarnation, cross, resurrection, (and coming of the Holy Spirit). Here three of the rites permit variations according to the season. Then the people join in the angelic hymn "Holy, holy, holy". This is followed by a section corresponding to the "Hear us" of the 1662 book—which in the Taizé rite is a full epiclesis—and the narrative of the institution. There follows an anamnesis, a prayer that God will accept what we offer, and the doxology.

4. *The Breaking of the Bread*

With or without public prayer the Bread is now broken, though in two of the rites this act is preceded by the Lord's Prayer.

5. *The Communion*

With or without the Lord's Prayer or other preparatory prayers, the consecrated bread and wine are shared.

6. *The Dismissal*

After a short prayer of gratitude and self-dedication (and, in the African and English rites, the optional use of *Gloria in excelsis*), the people are told to go forth. Three of the rites contain a Blessing for those who wish to use it, but it is obligatory only in that of Taizé.

These four new rites suggest that the 1958 Lambeth Conference was right to think that a basic pattern could be found for the Eucharist. The pattern did not need to be elaborated by any special committee, as appears from the fact that the Taizé rite is so closely similar in outline to the three which are Anglican. The fact is that those who produced the rites drew on a common fund of scholarship and read the same books, of which one of the most important has been Father Josef Jungmann's *Missarum Sollemnia*.[12]

[12] This book was published in German in 1949, and English editions have since been published by Benziger Brothers Inc., New York, with the title *The Mass of the Roman Rite: Its Origins and Development.*

"The machinery for discipline has broken down", said the Royal Commission in 1906. Little has happened in the past sixty years which would have made them alter their opinion. Churchmen of both Evangelical and Anglo-Catholic traditions have grown accustomed to their proprietary deviations from the text of the old Prayer Book. Now in 1967 there is a need to examine once more what liturgical obedience should mean, both in relation to a society which rejects authoritarianism, and in its theological perspective as a framework for unity and love. The deliberate flexibility of the new rites will greatly help us to interpret our new forms of obedience, and there is no fear that we are entering a new mock-Tudor period of imposed uniformity.

And against the sixty years of indiscipline we can gratefully set sixty equal years of advancing scholarship, and thirty in which this scholarship has found its way into pastoral practice through the Liturgical Movement and, among Anglicans, the Parish Communion. This is a time of hope.

It is not a time for complacency. For the same social change which demands a reinterpretation of obedience calls also for a careful examination of the way we present our liturgy. To some extent this will depend on a critical assessment of our different traditions of ceremonial, for it is unlikely that all the details of Byzantine court etiquette will remain expressive in the context of our own twentieth-century megalopolis. More urgently still, we need to see how the emerging pattern of the liturgy can best be clothed in language. All over the world Anglicans are agitating for the use of modern language in the liturgy, and it is only too evident that the four recent liturgies have been unable to meet this demand, though it should be added that none of the examples of "modern English" so far produced has attracted much approval. The question of language demands urgent study and action, and it is one of the most difficult of the tasks ahead of those who are revising the liturgy.

Another weakness in the present Anglican position is its lack of one clear basic doctrine of the Eucharist. The Lambeth statement about the eucharistic sacrifice was a step in the right direction, but its implications have gone largely unheeded, as was clear in the Church Assembly's recent debates about the new English rite.

These debates were not concerned with the 1928 problems about the epiclesis, for the simple reason that the draft rite did not contain one. But they concentrated their discussion on some words in the anamnesissection of the prayer of consecration, which read:

> Wherefore, O Lord, having in remembrance his [Christ's] saving passion, his resurrection from the dead, and his glorious ascension into heaven, and looking for the coming of his kingdom, we offer unto thee this bread and this cup. . . .

When these words first became known they provoked a strong reaction amongst Conservative Evangelicals, who felt not only that the words "we offer unto thee this bread and this cup" were obscure in meaning, but that they might easily lead towards an undesirable doctrine of the eucharistic sacrifice. For a time it seemed as if the Church of England would be trapped in deadlock as bitter and unproductive as that of forty years before. The Conservative Evangelicals produced a counter-proposal, in the knowledge that for at least some of the Anglo-Catholics it would be theologically acceptable. For a time discussion was shelved, while a committee tried to find a formula on which all would agree. But the attempt proved vain, and the Convocations decided to adopt the very solution which Frere, forty years before, had suggested for the problem of the epiclesis. They sanctioned both the original text and also, as an alternative, the Evangelical proposal "we give thanks to thee over this bread and this cup". The irony of the debate was, as the Archbishop of Canterbury said from the chair, that biblical scholarship seemed to be showing more and more clearly that the two texts in fact meant the same.

In the event the House of Laity refused to accept the Convocations' decision because they objected to the use of alternatives in the consecration prayer. The text of the *Second Series* rite now authorized for use has an anamnesis with strong similarities to the one in the first English Prayer Book of 1549. This text was accepted not as an ideal solution, but as a compromise. By the time the *Second Series* Holy Communion comes back for reconsideration by the Church Assembly, the possibilities for the anamnesis will have been officially studied, and it is to be hoped that the issues involved will be more clearly defined than they were in the recent debates.

This new rite has solved important questions about the basic eucharistic pattern. It has provided a new and hopeful context for liturgical discipline. But the work of experiment has still to be done. We have yet to discover whether it will contribute to a clearer understanding of the Eucharist among the Christians—and the non-Christians—of this generation.

7

EUCHARISTIC THEOLOGY
TODAY

C. B. NAYLOR

In the second edition of *Corpus Christi* (1965) E. L. Mascall attributes the recent rapprochment between differing traditions in eucharistic theology not only to the charitable atmosphere in which contemporary debate is conducted, but also to the considerable advances made in theological thinking on "both sides". So considerable have been these advances that a thorough revision of his original book was found necessary within ten years of its publication. This is a period of remarkable fluidity in eucharistic thought and practice, and there are several reasons for this state of affairs.

Eucharistic theology now finds itself somewhere in the confluence of three movements—liturgical, biblical, and ecumenical. Liturgical studies have penetrated behind the barriers set up by medieval and post-medieval ways of thinking to a dynamic view of the Eucharist, varied in practice and extensive in meaning. The Eucharist is action; the liturgy something done and experienced: and the theology is bound up with the action and the experience. Similarly the Liturgical Movement, which aims to restore the Eucharist to the centre of parish life as a congregational concern in action and discussion, has helped to bring at least some aspects of eucharistic theology within range of the ordinary worshipper. It is true that congregational practice has sometimes contrived some questionable theology, especially in connection with the offertory procession, but this is at least an error of liturgical enthusiasm.

In its turn biblical theology has extended the scope and liveliness of eucharistic theology by exploring its biblical context in both Old and New Testaments. The notion of sacrifice, for example, has been rescued from its limited preoccupation with death into a wider and more positive affirmation which includes offering, communion, covenant, and renewal. This provides a broader area in which the vexed question of eucharistic sacrifice can be discussed. In New Testament studies the actions and words of the Last Supper have been subjected to detailed scrutiny and considerable discussion devoted to their sacrificial character, Passover associations, and eschatological significance. Notable, too, has been the recovery of the biblical meaning of memorial or anamnesis, and of the Jewish thanksgiving, or blessing, as inclusive of consecration, or as drawing elements so blessed into the realm of God's acts in creation and redemption for which thanksgiving is offered. These and other biblical insights, contributed and shared by churches of different theological traditions, provide categories of communication which make ecumenical interchange of ideas possible and fruitful. And here the Ecumenical Movement is at work, urging this exchange of ideas, especially when it finds its way forward blocked at the very point where Christian unity should be expressed and realized—in the Eucharist. But already much of the fear and prejudice of the past has been dispelled as a result of co-operation in conference, service, and witness, and to a certain degree in worship. The story of the Faith and Order Movement from Edinburgh 1927 to Montreal 1964 bears heartening testimony to this.

In a period of such fluidity and of so many cross-currents in eucharistic thought, one may be excused some diffidence in trying to assess the present situation. But within the limits of a chapter it would seem wise to be content with selecting two developments which appear important. One is of ancient lineage, the other less notorious. The first is the familiar problem of the "eucharistic sacrifice"—a term which has so divided western Christendom during the last four hundred years, and which even in these days of greater mutual understanding can revive the controversial fears of the past. This was very evident in the recent earnest debate in the joint session of the Convocations of Canterbury and York over the sentence in the proposed revision of the Holy Communion service, "we offer unto thee this bread and this cup". Nevertheless the distance through which Catholic and Protestant theologians have moved towards each other in recent years has been admirably described by E. L. Mascall in the second edition of *Corpus Christi* to which allusion has already been made. He deals on the Catholic side principally with the theories of de la Taille, Vonier, Masure, and Journet: on the Protestant side with Benoît, Leenhardt, Thurian, Aulén and D. M. Baillie. In the first part of *Eucharist and Sacrifice*, G. Aulén covers similar ground, including reference to Hebert, Dix, and A. M. Ramsey. A shorter essay on the same subject is to be found in *Studia Liturgica* II, 2 by A. M. Allchin. This is of particular interest because he deals with the theology of R. G. Prenter (Lutheran, Denmark) which is little known in this country. It would be presumptuous and unnecessary to attempt to present yet a further analysis, but one or two reflections may be in order.

In the first place it is notable that on "both sides" the understanding of Christ's sacrifice is extended to include the whole life from incarnation through ministry, death, and resurrection to the ascension. H. A. Hageman of the Dutch Reformed Church in the United States and a prominant figure in the World Council of Churches in *Pulpit and Table* traces the inadequacy of much Reformed eucharistic worship to the almost exclusive concentration upon the Crucifixion, and Atonement. "In some parts of the Netherlands it was even the custom to attend the annual Communion in mourning. We have not lost this trait. Many a Reformed or Presbyterian congregation would find a Christmas or Easter Communion almost a contradiction."[1] M. Thurian, the distinguished Reformed theologian of Taizé, writes in *Eucharistic Memorial*,[2] "When it performs this showing forth of the sacrifice of the cross in union with the showing forth by the Son before the Father, the Church makes the memorial of the entire redemptive work of Christ." He refers with approval to the historic eastern liturgies which "set before the Father all that the Son has accomplished from his conception in Mary to his entry into the heavenly sanctuary". By this the liturgy intends to "fling us into the total mystery of Christ which becomes present through the Eucharist". The same larger conception of the sacrifice of Christ is to be found also in Roman Catholic writers. E. L. Mascall quotes[3] from Journet (*La Messe*) where the sacrifice includes the passion, death, resurrection, and ascension. Whatever we may think of Odo Casel's mystery

---

[1] *Pulpit and Table*, p. 116.
[2] M. Thurian, *Eucharistic Memorial*, Part 2, pp. 38, 9.
[3] Op. cit., p. 148-9.

theology, it is clear that he understands what is re-presented in the Eucharist to be the whole mystery of Christ. "What is meant is that the whole oiconomia, the whole design of salvation from the incarnation to the parousia . . . does take on a sacramental presence". And "In the eucharist the passion of Christ is present . . . but the passion can in no way be taken out of the context of the whole saving action."[4]

This richer, dynamic interpretation of the sacrifice recalled in the Eucharist is in line, and frequently connected with a much enlarged and extended concept of sacrifice that has been the fruit of Old Testament and anthropological studies. Whether we think of sacrifice in terms of offering/immolation: transformation/impartation (Masure) or covenant/cleansing: communion/glorification (Dillistone) these constitute a process, a drama, a movement enacted through the rite, in the course of which it is impossible to single out one moment as "*the* sacrifice". This favours a dramatic understanding of the eucharistic rite which is less inclined to pinpoint moments as determinative. "The liturgy as a whole, not one moment only or sentence, is the transcending event which deeply transfigures the life of the Body as a whole."[5] Further, with the recovery of a doctrine of sacrifice that does justice to the whole complex of events which compose it, it is possible for differing emphases to stand together, no longer seen as in opposition, but as complementary within the wider whole. But mutual recognition and acceptance are necessary for a comprehension of the complete doctrine.

Secondly, on "both sides" there has been a thorough investigation into the relation between the historic sacrifice of Christ (with its wider interpretation) and what goes on in the Eucharist. On the Catholic side there is whole-hearted determination to rebut the charge that the once-for-all sacrifice is taught as repeated in the Mass; with equal determination many Protestants are anxious to avoid the conclusion that the Eucharist is a bare memorial, whether by word or symbol, of a past and distant event. Here one is bound to record the debt owed to F. W. Dillistone for his penetrating

---

4 O. Casel, *The Mystery of Christian Worship*, (ed. B. Neunheuser) pp. 151, 152, 154.

5 N. A. Nissiotis, "Worship, Eucharist and Intercommunion" in *Studia Liturgica* II. 3.

study into the nature of the symbol.[6] His disclosure of its evocative and mediatory power in the individual and social experience, in culture and religion, warns us that any use of the term "symbol", especially in connexion with the sacrament, must take account of the whole range of significance and potency that may be contained in whatever we may rightly be described by that term.

From the Catholic side the way forward has been pointed by the work of A. Vonier, E. Masure, and C. Journet, in particular in a reappraisal of the term "sacrament". By this means it is maintained that the historic sacrifice is not repeated. It is the same sacrifice made present through the "efficacious sign" or the sacramental causality of the symbol that Christ ordained. "The creative power of symbols," wrote Vonier in *Doctrine of the Eucharist*, "the productive efficacy of signs, the incredible resourcefulness of simple things in the hand of God to produce spiritual realities, nay to reproduce their historic setting, this is the sacramental world, and it is profoundly unlike any other world."[7] In the words of Masure, "The sacramental sign is efficacious because it has been instituted by our Lord".[8] Through the sacrament we are brought into a sacramental world with its own laws of causality, dependent entirely on the word of Christ. In such a world there can be no question of a repetition of Calvary. It is the same once-for-all sacrifice that is actualized.

On the Protestant side the way forward from the bare notion of mental recollection or rehearsal seems to lie along the line of the Old Testament conception of a rite as actualizing past events by their recollection and dramatic representation. Within the context of the rite the anamnesis is a true recalling of the salvation event that is proclaimed. (J. D. Benoît, J. Leenhardt, M. Thurian). This interpretation of anamnesis has been severely challenged,[9] but the extent of its appeal can be judged by its adoption in the Whiteley Lectures (Baptist) for 1962, given by S. F. Winward.[10] "The celebration of the Passover was no mere mental recollection of an event long since

[6] *Christianity and Symbolism.*

[7] Op. cit., p. 35.

[8] *The Christian Sacrifice* p. 225.

[9] D. Jones, *J.T.S.*, October 1955. N. Hook, *The Eucharist in the N. T.*, p. 144ff.

[10] *The Reformation of our worship*, p. 48.

past. It was a here and now participation in the saving event commemorated, an event with abiding consequences and pregnant with promise. In the Eucharist Christ is present, and the saving event is contemporary and operative . . . The Eucharist is a sacrifice because *the* sacrifice is present."[11]

This brief and rough summary does scant justice to the full and rich expositions of eucharistic sacrifice in these authors, or to the variety of their treatment. It would be unrealistic to minimize differences. It is of course still possible to recognize the persistence of the different lines of tradition such as are so clearly summarized in *Christianity and Symbolism* (chapter 9); but it is equally possible to detect movement away from the more rigid traditions described by Dr Dillistone as Roman and Jerusalemite, towards the more flexible Greek and Hebraic traditions. But differences become articulate in debate. There is, for example, the question—"Who or what is offered in the Eucharist? Ourselves or Christ or his sacrifice?" E. L. Mascall believes the solution to lie in a recognition of the unity between Christ and the members (through Baptism) of his body, and of the reality of his sacrifice in the sacrament, so that we may say "The whole Christ offers the whole Christ", and, he adds, "we should leave the matter at that".[12] D. M. Baillie on the other hand affirmed that "we can only make an offering in union with Christ's eternal sacrifice", and "in the sacrament Christ being truly present he unites us by faith with his eternal sacrifice so that we may plead and receive its benefits and offer ourselves in prayer and praise to God".[13] There is a serious difference here which A. M. Allchin tries to overcome by suggesting that "we offer Christ" is really a way of expressing "we are drawn into his sacrifice". But C. F. D. Moule points the real difference where at the conclusion of his study entitled *The Sacrifice of Christ*, he writes: "Communion" or "fellowship" (κοινωνία), "together with" (συν-), and "in Christ" (ἐν Χριστῷ)—these, as I see it, are the keys to the meaning of the Eucharistic sacrifice; and they express a union not of identity but of fellowship".[14] The problem seems to be one of trying to reconcile differing, but not wholly opposing categories of thought in which to

11 Cf. N. A. Nissiotis, *Studia Liturgica* II, 3, p. 207.
12 op. cit., p. 183; cf. G. Dix *The Shape of the Liturgy*, p. 251.
13 *The Theology of the Sacraments*, p. 118.
14 Op. cit., p. 58.

express the reality of personal unity, when we speak of Christ and his Church.

A corollary to this debate may point in the direction of the area which needs to be explored further if a solution is to be found. Some theologians insist that a doctrine of the Church which upholds the absolute unity of Christ the Head with the members of his Body (*totus Christus*), together with the reality and presence of Christ's sacrifice in the Eucharist, guarantees a doctrine of the uniqueness and completeness of Christ's sacrifice, and is a safeguard against Pelagianism. To say "we offer Christ" in the Eucharist is the only sure way in which we can avoid claiming the right to offer anything of our own merit.[15] This concern to guarantee the sole sufficiency of Christ's sacrifice, and to eschew any implication of merit, or suggestion of Pelagianism, is a marked feature of contemporary discussion, and finds expression in other ways than that referred to above. In a definition of sacrifice in which he is concerned to give due priority to the action of God, in order to correct the Godward exaggeration in certain theses, F. W. Dillistone writes: "It may be objected that in this definition insufficient attention is paid to man's part in the sacrificial action." The author answers this objection by attributing the initiative in all human thought, reflection, and action involved in true worship to the activity of the Holy Spirit. "In all of this, it is the Holy Spirit who is inwardly at work."[16] At this point one is reminded of the persistent emphasis laid upon the sovereign action of the Holy Spirit in the Eucharist by contemporary Orthodox writers. It is the Holy Spirit who effects the reality of the sacrifice in the Eucharist, and whose transforming power is operative there as in the whole history of redemption which includes Pentecost and the Baptism of every Christian believer. The Eucharist is even described as an offering by the Paraclete to the Father's throne (N. A. Nissiotis). Again, the whole sacramental and eucharistic life of the Church persists in a *Pentecôte continuée* (B. Bobrinsky). "The epiclesis," wrote G. E. Oulton "in the eastern

---

[15] See Jardine Grisbroke—an Orthodox theologian—in *Studia Liturgica* II, 2, in connection with A. M. Ramsey's warning about the "Offertory" in *Durham Essays and Addresses*.

[16] Op. cit., p. 260.

tradition is a climax, a more intense and solemn invoking of him in whom the entire action is carried on."[17]

In contrast with this it is instructive to read in a Roman Catholic critique of the Liturgical Constitution of the Second Vatican Council a severe comment upon the all but complete absence of reference to the Holy Spirit in the document. P. Vanberger, the critic, compares this with the Faith and Order Report on Worship belonging to the same year. The Report frequently underlines the action of the Holy Spirit in the liturgy and in every part of the Church's life. In a footnote Vanberger seems to connect the absence of pneumatology in the document with the dominance of Christology and a weakness in ecclesiology that are characteristic of the Liturgical Movement in the Roman Catholic Church. It may be that a way further through our denominational differences lies in an investigation into this very criticism. What, for example, is the distinction between describing the Church as the body of Christ and as the fellowship of the Spirit? There seems to be a curious discrepancy between the almost formal references to the Spirit in some eucharistic theologies and the lavish references in others.

The second theme that calls for mention concerns the relation between word and sacrament in the Eucharist. Here again we see the influence of the biblical, liturgical, and ecumenical movements. The remarkable revival of biblical theology in the Roman Catholic Church was bound to raise questions about the place of the Ministry of the Word in the liturgy. "We can understand," wrote L. Bouyer in *Life and Liturgy* (1956), "how much there is to deplore in the present state of the *Missa Catechumenorum*. In the first place the whole groundwork has been shaken out of place by the almost complete disappearance of the readings from the Old Testament. Then, the suppression of the *lectio continua*, the full and continuous reading of the Books of the Bible, has now obscured the complete and unified significance of all the lessons which made the Mystery the key to the whole of sacred history."[18] In its turn the Liturgical Movement which, among other things, seeks, by a careful production of the service, to illuminate the meaning of each part and stage in the liturgy, was bound sooner or later to face the question how or

17 *The Holy Spirit and Holy Communion*, p. 112.
18 Op. cit., p. 113.

why the Ministry of the Word precedes the Ministry of the Sacrament. Again, the Ecumenical Movement has created an atmosphere of liturgical comparison and denominational self-examination. S. M. Gibbard in an article quotes K. Barth "What we know today as the church service both in Roman Catholicism *and* in Protestantism is a torso. The Roman Catholic Church has a sacramental service without preaching. . . . We have a service with a sermon but without sacraments. Both types of service are impossible."[19] That was written nearly thirty years ago.

In official and semi-official statements we may detect a common concern for the integration of word and sacrament in the liturgy. "Sacred Scripture is of the greatest importance in the celebration of the liturgy." "The sermon should draw its content mainly from spiritual sources, and its character should be that of proclamation of God's wonderful works in the history of salvation, the mystery of Christ ever made present and active within us, especially in the celebration of the liturgy." "The treasures of the Bible are to be opened up more lavishly so that a richer fare may be provided for the faithful at the *table of God's word*" (italics not in the original). These are quotations from the Roman Catholic Constitution on the Liturgy (1963). A Faith and Order study on the Eucharist conducted in 1965 by representatives from the Anglican, Lutheran, Methodist, Orthodox, Reformed, and United Churches, with three Roman Catholic consultants, stated among its conclusions: "The proclamation of the Word of God . . . quickens faith in those who are to communicate at the Lord's Table. We therefore submit that in contrast to the frequent and harmful separation between Word and Sacrament, there should be no celebration of the Eucharist that does not include the Ministry of the Word".

It is significant that the twelfth Irish Liturgical Conference (Roman Catholic) of 1965 took as its theme "The Liturgy of the Word—Impact and Problems". In the course of its proceedings the intimate relationship between word and sacrament was underlined, the former described as stirring up and deepening faith necessary for participation in the Eucharist. In the Orthodox theology of N. A. Nissiotis the liturgy of the word finds its realization in the sacrament. The preached word is the proclamation of the gospel whose

---

[19] Karl Barth, *The Knowledge of God and the Service of God*, 1938, p. 211.

message of salvation and reconciliation is actualized in the Eucharist. The word is an effective and necessary preparation for the representation of the victorious, saving events, whose proclamation finds its fulfilment in the Eucharist.

In the two distinguished Roman Catholic theologians, L. Bouyer and K. Rahner, a powerful theology of the Word dominates their treatment of this theme. "Of course the Mystery is not only "word" —in so far as for men "word" can be opposed to "deed" or to "being". But since the Mystery is a personal love that desires to communicate itself to living persons, it must be accepted by us first of all under the aspect of word; and the other implications of the Mystery can be revealed to us only in dependence on this primary aspect."[20] In Karl Rahner the word as proclaimed in the Church makes present the saving events it declares. The word is effective in various ways and at different levels but finds its supreme actualisation in the sacrament. All expressions of the word meet and derive their meaning and power from, and lead up to, the sacramental Word through which the Lord is present in the Eucharist.

From the Protestant side we have a different approach in the writing of H. A. Hageman. Here the need is not to restore the theology and practice of a neglected part of one service, but to bring together what had become two distinct services. In *Pulpit and Table* the writer links past neglect of the sacrament with an earlier unbiblical dualism between what appealed to the mind, and what appealed to the senses, with its consequent intellectualization of public worship which would find no place for the sacrament. But further thought reveals that neglect of the sacrament was in fact the cause of this unbiblical misunderstanding of the word. "Could we have so easily dissolved the Word of God, that concrete and real event into a set of abstractions true for all times and places, if every proclamation of the Word had been followed by the concrete and real event of the breaking of the bread?" There is more to follow. "Could the Reformed churches have proved such fertile soil for the growth of sectarianism, producing one schism after another in their history, if every week they had reminded themselves that "We being many are one bread, and one body: for we are all partakers of that one bread? ... We have been slow to explore the connexion

---

[20] L. Bouyer, *Life and Liturgy*, p. 108.

between this unhappy tendency ("fissiparity") and our intellectuali-
sation of the gospel symbolised by our neglect of the sacrament."[21]

These are bold criticisms, part of which seems to suggest a
movement away from the familiar Reformed doctrine of a sacrament as sign and seal of God's word and promise. But the distance
between the argument of this book and that of the Catholic and
Orthodox interpretations quoted is pronounced. Nevertheless the
spirit of self-criticism and the will to explore and, if need be,
sacrifice "some of our most cherished traditions" (p. 115) is here and
elsewhere on "both sides" one of the hopeful signs and blessings of
the Ecumenical Movement. The willingness to break through the
impasse created by the controversies about the eucharistic sacrifice
is a penitent recognition of past theological errors and misunderstanding. This is theological advance, leading into questions about
the doctrine of the Church and the Holy Spirit. But the less
notorious question of the relation between word and sacrament
carries promise of theological advance no less fruitful. Whatever
answers are given to that question are likely ultimately to be
reflected in the liturgical form and practice of the Eucharist, and so
to influence the thought and life of those who share in the worship.
It is a question that seems to strike deep into the reasons for
differing human attitudes. It is a question that asks, among other
things, why whole sections of the Christian Church should for
many centuries have been dominated by the "word" and words; and
how near today are Catholic and Protestant writers in their interpretation of "the word". And when the word is related to the sacrament, what is the difference between saying "the proclamation of
the word is realized, or fulfilled, in the sacrament", and "the
sacrament is sign and seal of God's word"? These questions, coin-
ciding at a time when the whole field of communication and expression, language, word, image, symbol, ritual, and drama, is being
widely explored, may well lead into new avenues of theological
study. In any case, the recovery of due emphases in the inseparable
parts of the service, in liturgical practice and theological consideration, must lead to an enrichment and enlargement of the Church's
understanding of the Eucharist.

[21] Op. cit., pp. 114, 5.